Great Escapes
Asia

Texts by Christiane Reiter   *Edited by* Angelika Taschen

Great Escapes
Asia

TASCHEN

HONG KONG KÖLN LONDON LOS ANGELES MADRID PARIS TOKYO

Red
Co

012 Gul Noor

022 Ananda

008 Dwarikas Hotel

Royal Desert Camp 032   ● 040 Narain Niwas Palace
Sardar Samand Palace 054 ●   046 Samode Palace

Devi Garh 062 ●
072 Udai Bilas Palace

Road to Mandalay 146 ●
Bagan Hotel 152 ●   ● 138 Inle Princess
● 172 Fou
The Strand Hotel 160 ●

Nilaya Hermitage 080 ●

Green Magic Nature Resort 088 ●

Eastern & Oriental Express 166 ●

Shalimar Spice Garden Resort 096 ●
Houseboat 104 ●

128 Ulpotha
The Sun House 110 ●
Taprobane Island 118 ●

The Datai 200 ●
Cheong Fatt Tze Mansion 194 ●

A journey of a 1,000 miles begins with the first step.
Chinese proverb

Losari Coffee Plantation

Contents Inhalt Sommaire

Price categories:		Preiskategorien:		Catégories de prix:	
$	up to 150 US$	$	bis 150 US$	$	jusqu'à 150 US$
$$	up to 250 US$	$$	bis 250 US$	$$	jusqu'à 250 US$
$$$	up to 450 US$	$$$	bis 450 US$	$$$	jusqu'à 450 US$
$$$$	over 450 US$	$$$$	über 450 US$	$$$$	plus de 450 US$

Living Like in a Museum...
Dwarika's Hotel, Kathmandu

Living Like in a Museum

If Dwarika Das Shrestha hadn't been so fond of jogging, this hotel would probably not exist. One morning in 1952 this young Nepalese man was running through the streets of Kathmandu and past a construction site where a carpenter was in the midst of sawing through a splendidly carved pillar. But before he got the chance to turn the individual pieces into firewood, Dwarika Das Shrestha had them put back together and installed the pillar in his own garden. This spontaneous rescue of the old pillar marked the start of his life's work: Up until his death in 1992 Dwarika Das Shrestha collected Nepalese handcrafted art and used it to adorn Dwarika's Hotel. Guests at the house today live in a building with 74 individually decorated rooms. Here a window from the sixteenth century, there a hand-painted curtain. One moment you are stepping through a richly adorned wooden doorway and the next into an idyllic inner courtyard with terracotta tiles. Dwarika's is like a mosaic of Nepalese art and culture. It is a hotel with all the comforts one could wish for at the start of the third millennium and at the same time a fascinating museum that offers the opportunity to directly experience the ancient history of an entire country.

Books to pack: "Touching my father's Soul. A Sherpa's Journey to the top of Everest" by Jamling Tenzing Norgay

Dwarika's Hotel	
P.O. Box 459, Battisputali	
Kathmandu, Nepal	
Tel. +977 (1) 447 07 70 and 447 94 88	
Fax +977 (1) 447 13 79 and 447 83 78	
Email: info@dwarikas.com	
Website: www.dwarikas.com	
www.great-escapes-hotels.com	

DIRECTIONS	5 minutes from the airport and 10 minutes from the city centre of Kathmandu.
RATES	$$
ROOMS	69 standard rooms and 5 suites – all individually furnished.
FOOD	Nepalese menus in the main restaurant "Krishnarpan", international cuisine in "Toran" restaurant, snacks in the "Fusion Bar".
HISTORY	Opened in 1970, furnished with centuries-old handcrafted art, in 1980 received the PATA Heritage Award.
X-FACTOR	Living like in a museum – but without having to whisper.

Wohnen wie im Museum

Wäre Dwarika Das Shrestha nicht so gerne joggen gegangen – es gäbe dieses Hotel vielleicht gar nicht. An einem Morgen des Jahres 1952 lief der junge Nepali durch die Straßen Kathmandus und an einer Baustelle vorbei, auf der ein Zimmermann gerade eine prachtvoll geschnitzte Säule mittendurch sägte. Doch noch bevor er die Einzelteile zu Feuerholz machen konnte, ließ Dwarika Das Shrestha die Stücke wieder zusammenfügen und stellte die neue alte Säule in seinem eigenen Garten auf. Es war eine Spontanrettung, aus der eine Lebensaufgabe wurde: Bis zu seinem Tod 1992 sammelte Dwarika Das Shrestha nepalesische Handwerkskunst – und schuf mit ihrer Hilfe Dwarika's Hotel. Wer das Haus heute besucht, wohnt in einem der 74 Zimmer, von denen jedes ein anderes Gesicht zeigt. Hier sieht man ein Fenster aus dem 16. Jahrhundert, dort einen handbemalten Vorhang, einmal tritt man durch eine reich verzierte Holztür, ein andermal in einen idyllischen Innenhof mit Terrakottafliesen. Dwarika's ist wie ein Mosaik nepalesischer Kunst und Kultur. Es ist ein Hotel mit allem Komfort, den man sich zu Beginn des 3. Jahrtausends wünscht, und zugleich ein faszinierendes Museum mit allen Möglichkeiten, die uralte Geschichte eines ganzen Landes unmittelbar zu erleben.

Buchtipps: »Auf den Spuren meines Vaters. Die Sherpas und der Everest« von Jamling Tenzing Norgay

Habiter comme dans un musée

Si Dwarika Das Shrestha n'avait pas autant aimé faire du footing, cet hôtel n'existerait peut-être pas. Un matin de 1952, le jeune Népalais courait dans les rues de Katmandou quand il passa près d'un chantier et vit un charpentier sciant en son milieu une colonne en bois superbement sculptée. Mais avant que ce dernier ne s'avise d'en faire du bois à brûler, Dwarika Das Shrestha assembla les morceaux et installa la colonne dans son jardin. Ce sauvetage spontané fut le début d'une passion qui allait durer toute sa vie : jusqu'à sa mort en 1992 Dwarika Das Shrestha collectionna une multitude d'objets artisanaux népalais au moyen desquels il créa le Dwarika's Hotel. Aujourd'hui le client réside dans l'une des 74 chambres qui toutes montrent un visage différent. Dans celle-ci il trouvera une fenêtre datant du 16ᵉ siècle, dans celle-là un rideau peint à la main. A un endroit il pourra admirer une porte en bois richement décorée, à un autre, une petite cour idyllique avec son carrelage en terre cuite. Le Dwarika's est une mosaïque de l'art et de la culture du Népal. Proposant tout le confort que l'on peut souhaiter en ce début du troisième millénaire, il est en même temps un musée fascinant qui nous fait découvrir l'histoire ancestrale de tout un pays.

Livre à emporter : « L'Eveil du Bouddha » de Tom Lowenstein

ANREISE	5 Fahrtminuten vom Flughafen und 10 Fahrtminuten vom Stadtzentrum Kathmandus entfernt.
PREIS	$$
ZIMMER	69 Zimmer und 5 Suiten – alle individuell ausgestattet.
KÜCHE	Nepalesische Menüs im Restaurant »Krishnarpan«, internationale Küche im »Toran«, Snacks in der »Fusion Bar«.
GESCHICHTE	1970 eröffnet, ausgestattet mit jahrhundertealter Handwerkskunst, 1980 mit dem PATA Heritage Award ausgezeichnet.
X-FAKTOR	Wohnen wie im Museum – aber ohne steife Flüsteratmosphäre.

ACCÈS	Situé à 5 min en voiture de l'aéroport et à 10 min du centre-ville de Katmandou.
PRIX	$$
CHAMBRES	69 chambres et 5 suites – aménagement individuel.
RESTAURATION	Menus népalais au « Krishnarpan », cuisine internationale au « Toran », snacks au « Fusion Bar ».
HISTOIRE	Ouvert en 1970, aménagé avec des objets artisanaux vieux de plusieurs siècles, a été doté du prix PATA Heritage Award en 1980.
LE « PETIT PLUS »	Habiter comme dans un musée – l'atmosphère feutrée en moins.

A Dream of Paradise...
Gul Noor, Dal Lake, Kashmir

A Dream of Paradise

These photos show a paradise and at the same time one of the most dangerous locations in the world, because the Dal Lake, this picture-book water against the backdrop of the Himalayas, is near Srinagar in Kashmir. The civil war that escalated there in the late 1980s has already cost 10 000 people their lives and created a country, which for travellers, contains an incalculable risk. There is not much alternative but to just dream that one is there and at least board one of the houseboats anchored in Dal Lake in your mind's eye. These floating palaces owe their existence to the British who came to Kashmir in the late nineteenth century and wanted to settle there. When the maharaja prohibited them from buying property, they simply moved their residences onto the water. Today one of the most beautiful of the boats which have been converted into hotels is the "Gul Noor", a fantasia of hand-carved cedar wood planks, Victorian-inspired furniture, shining pewter and sparkling crystal. If you sit on the veranda, which overlooks the sea like a lodge, you experience a deluxe nature spectacle, bathe in the sunshine and watch the "shikaras" – small gondolas which add a touch of Venice to Dal Lake. They are mobile kiosks that the peddlers use to glide from boat door to boat door selling food, spices or flowers. The sad thing about dreams is that you can't smell in them – otherwise you would now be wrapped in the fragrance of these flowers.

**Book to pack: "Goat: A Story of Kashmir and Notting Hill"
by Justine Hardy**

Gul Noor

Kashmir Houseboat Booking

3/4, Windsor Mansion, Janpath Lane

New Delhi – 110001, India

Tel. +91 (11) 23 35 32 08

Fax +91 (11) 23 32 39 06

Email: request@kashmir-houseboat-booking.com

Website: www.kashmir-houseboat-booking.com

www.great-escapes-hotels.com

DIRECTIONS	The Dal Lake is situated on the northeast edge of Srinagar, 25 km / 16 miles from the airport.
RATES	$
ROOMS	A living room, bedroom, bath, kitchen and a veranda. A "boat boy" and a "shikara" gondola are included.
FOOD	Three meals are served daily featuring dishes from Kashmir.
HISTORY	In 1888 the British built the first houseboat.
X-FACTOR	As if one could simply float away from all the political problems.

Der Traum vom Paradies

Diese Fotos zeigen ein Paradies. Und zugleich einen der gefährlichsten Brennpunkte der Welt – denn der Dal-See, dieser Bilderbuchsee vor der Kulisse des Himalaja, liegt bei Srinagar in Kaschmir. Der Bürgerkrieg, der dort Ende der achtziger Jahre eskalierte, hat bereits zehntausende Menschen das Leben gekostet und ein Land hinterlassen, das für Reisende ein unberechenbares Risiko birgt. Es bleibt einem nicht viel mehr, als sich dorthin zu träumen und wenigstens in Gedanken an Bord eines der Hausboote zu gehen, die im Dal-See vor Anker liegen. Zu verdanken sind diese schwimmenden Paläste den Briten, die Ende des 19. Jahrhunderts nach Kaschmir kamen und sich niederlassen wollten. Als der Maharadscha ihnen verbot, Grundstücke zu kaufen, verlegten sie ihre Wohnsitze einfach aufs Wasser – die Herkunft von einer Insel verpflichtet eben... Zu den schönsten Booten, die heute als Hotels dienen, gehört das »Gul Noor«, eine Phantasie aus handgeschnitzten Zedernholzbögen, viktorianisch inspirierten Möbeln, glänzendem Zinn und funkelndem Kristall. Wer auf der Veranda sitzt, die wie eine Loge auf den See hinausgeht, erlebt ein Naturschauspiel de luxe, badet im Sonnenschein und beobachtet die »Shikaras«, kleine Gondeln, die einen Hauch Venedig auf den Dal-See bringen. Sie sind mobile Kioske, mit denen die Händler von Bootstür zu Bootstür gleiten und Lebensmittel, Gewürze oder Blumen verkaufen. Das Traurige an Träumen ist, dass sie geruchlos bleiben – denn sonst würde einem jetzt der Duft dieser Blüten in die Nase steigen.

Buchtipp: »Die Farben der Hoffnung. Eine Geschichte aus Kaschmir und Notting Hill« von Justine Hardy

Rêver du paradis

Ces photos montrent un paradis, mais en même temps l'un des endroits les plus dangereux du monde car le lac de Dal, un lac de toute beauté aux pieds de l'Himalaya, est situé près de Srinagar dans la région du Cachemire. La guerre civile, qui s'est envenimée à la fin des années quatre-vingts, a déjà coûté la vie à des milliers de personnes et a rendu le pays peu sûr pour les voyageurs. On se contentera donc de rêver en s'imaginant à bord de l'un de ces bateaux servant d'habitation, ancrés sur le lac de Dal. Ces palais flottants, on les doit aux Anglais qui, arrivés au Cachemire à la fin du 19e siècle, voulurent s'y installer. Lorsque le Maharadjah leur interdit d'acheter des terres, ils établirent tout simplement leur domicile sur l'eau – ils n'étaient pas des insulaires pour rien... Parmi les plus beaux « houseboats », qui aujourd'hui font office d'hôtels, il faut signaler le « Gul Noor », un délire d'arcs en bois de cèdre sculptés à la main, de meubles d'inspiration victorienne, d'étains brillants et de cristal étincelant. Le visiteur assis sur la véranda, qui s'avance vers le lac comme une loge de théâtre, assiste à un spectacle grandiose. Caressé par les rayons du soleil, il observera aussi les « shikaras », des petites gondoles qui donnent au lac de Dal un petit air de Venise. Les commerçants qui se trouvent à bord vont de bateau en bateau pour vendre de la nourriture, des épices ou des fleurs. Le plus triste avec les rêves, c'est qu'ils sont inodores. Dommage pour toutes les senteurs qui accompagnent les bateaux.

Livre à emporter : « Du Cachemire à Kaboul » d'Omar Khan

ANREISE	Der Dal-See liegt am Nordostrand von Srinagar, 25 km vom Flughafen entfernt.	
PREIS	$	
ZIMMER	Wohn- und Schlafzimmer, Bad, Küche und Veranda. »Boat Boy« und »Shikara«-Gondel inklusive.	
KÜCHE	Täglich drei Mahlzeiten mit Gerichten aus Kaschmir.	
GESCHICHTE	1888 bauten Briten das erste Hausboot.	
X-FAKTOR	Als könnte man allen politischen Problemen davonschwimmen.	

ACCÈS	Le lac de Dal est situé au nord-est de Srinagar, à 25 km de l'aéroport.
PRIX	$
CHAMBRES	Salle à manger et chambre, salle de bains, cuisine et véranda, « boat boy » et gondole « shikara » compris.
CUISINE	Trois repas par jour comprenant des spécialités.
HISTOIRE	Le premier bateau fut construit en 1888 par les Anglais.
LE « PETIT PLUS »	Naviguer loin de tous les conflits.

Everything Flows...
Ananda - In the Himalayas, Uttaranchal

Ananda – Uttaranchal, In the Himalayas

Everything Flows

Vata, Pitta and Kapha can easily come out of balance in the stress of everyday life. What could make you happier than putting these physical energies back into balance with the help of Ayurveda therapy in one of India's most beautiful hotels? The Ananda, in the Himalayas, truly deserves the term "health temple" like no other. Situated against the cinematic backdrop of the Himalayas with a view across the valley of the Ganges, this white former maharaja's palace has a spa dedicated to Ayurveda for its guests. Okay, so the hard work of detoxification and purification is not always pleasurable, but afterwards one feels like one is wearing an eternal smile on one's face. One walks, as if on cotton wool, through the enchanting pavilions, the great ballroom or the winter garden and enjoys the peace in the rooms and suites. The Ananda Suite, for example, includes a private paradise garden, and the Vice-Regal Suite features a polished wooden floor, English antiques and a telescope to view the sparkling firmament over India. If, after days of meditation, you feel the need for an adrenalin kick then take a day trip on an elephant safari or a rafting tour of the Ganges.

Book to pack: "The Heart of God" by Rabindranath Tagore

Ananda – In the Himalayas

The Palace Estate
Narendra Nagar, District Tehri Garhwal
Uttaranchal – 249175, India
Tel. + 91 (1378) 22 75 00
Fax + 91 (1378) 22 75 50
Email: sales@anandaspa.com
Website: www.anandaspa.com
www.great-escapes-hotels.com

DIRECTIONS	Situated 260 km / 161 miles north of Delhi (transfer from Delhi via aircraft in 40 min. or by train & car in 5 hr.).
RATES	$$$$
ROOMS	70 luxury rooms, 3 Deluxe Suites, 1 Ananda Suite, 1 Vice-Regal Suite.
FOOD	5 restaurants with light "Ananda Spa Cuisine" and with fantastic views.
HISTORY	A former palace of the maharaja of Tehri Garhwal.
X-FACTOR	Everything is Ayurveda in one of the most beautiful spas in the world.

Alles im Fluss

Dass Vata, Pitta und Kapha aus dem Gleichgewicht geraten, kommt im Alltagsstress schnell einmal vor. Glücklich ist dann, wer diese Körperenergien mit Hilfe der Ayurvedatherapie und in einem der schönsten Hotels Indiens wieder ausbalancieren kann. Das Ananda – In the Himalayas verdient den Begriff »Wellness-Tempel« wie kaum ein anderes Haus. Vor der kinotauglichen Kulisse des Himalaja und mit Blick über das Tal des Ganges gelegen, lässt der weiße Palast die Zeiten der Maharadschas wieder aufleben und bittet seine Gäste in ein Spa, das sich dem Ayurveda verschrieben hat. Zugegeben: Entgiftung und Entschlackung sind nicht immer ganz angenehm – doch danach fühlt man sich, als trüge man auf ewig ein Lächeln im Gesicht. Wie auf Watte wandelt man durch die zauberhaften Pavillons, den großen Ballsaal oder den Wintergarten und genießt die Ruhe in den Zimmern und Suiten – zur Ananda Suite gehört beispielsweise ein eigener Paradiesgarten, und die Viceregal Suite bietet polierte Holzfußböden, britisch angehauchte Antiquitäten und ein Teleskop für den Blick in den glitzernden Sternenhimmel über Indien. Wer nach Tagen der Meditation wieder den Adrenalinkick sucht, plant einen Tagesausflug – eine Elefantensafari oder eine Raftingtour auf dem Ganges.

Buchtipp: »Das Herz Gottes« von Rabindranath Tagore

Le corps et l'âme en harmonie

Notre vie est un stress permanent, et que nous soyons de type vâta, pitta ou kapha, nous devons nous ressourcer. Heureux celui qui peut retrouver sa vitalité à l'aide de la médecine ayurvédique dans l'un des plus beaux hôtels de l'Inde.

Si l'un d'eux mérite la palme du bien-être, c'est bien l'Ananda Himalaya. Sur le décor grandiose des montagnes et avec vue sur la vallée du Gange, le palais blanc fait revivre l'époque des maharadjahs et offre à ses hôtes un centre de remise en forme voué à l'Ayurvéda.

Il faut bien sûr en passer par la désintoxication et la purification de l'organisme, ce qui n'a rien d'agréable, mais on se sent ensuite au septième ciel. Comme sur un nuage, on traverse les pavillons ravissants, la grande salle de bal ou le jardin d'hiver et on jouit du calme dans les chambres et les suites – la suite Ananda comprend par exemple un jardin particulier idyllique et la suite Viceregal offre des parquets polis, des antiquités « old England » et un télescope pour observer les étoiles au-dessus de l'Inde.

Si, après des jours passés à méditer, une envie d'action se fait sentir, il est possible de partir en excursion – en safari à dos d'éléphant ou en radeau sur le Gange.

Livre à emporter : « La demeure de la paix »
de Rabindranath Tagore

ANREISE	260 km nördlich von Delhi (Transfer von Delhi per Flugzeug in 40 min. oder per Zug & Auto in 5 h).
PREIS	$$$$
ZIMMER	70 Luxuszimmer, 3 Deluxe-Suiten, 1 Ananda-Suite, 1 Viceregal-Suite.
KÜCHE	5 Restaurants, darunter »The Restaurant« mit leichter »Ananda Spa Cuisine« und »The Tree Top Deck« mit traumhaftem Blick.
GESCHICHTE	Ein ehemaliger Palast auf dem Gelände des Maharadscha von Tehri Garhwal.
X-FAKTOR	Alles Ayurveda – in einem der schönsten Spas der Welt.

ACCÈS	Situé à 260 km au nord de Delhi (de Delhi par avion en 40 min ou par train et voiture en 5 h).
PRIX	$$$$
CHAMBRES	70 chambres, 3 suites, 1 suite Ananda, 1 suite Viceregal.
RESTAURATION	5 restaurants offrant une « Ananda Spa Cuisine » légère et un panorama sublime.
HISTOIRE	Situé dans l'enceinte du palais du maharadjah de Tehri Garhwal.
LE « PETIT PLUS »	Tout Ayurvéda – dans l'un des meilleurs centres de remise en forme du monde.

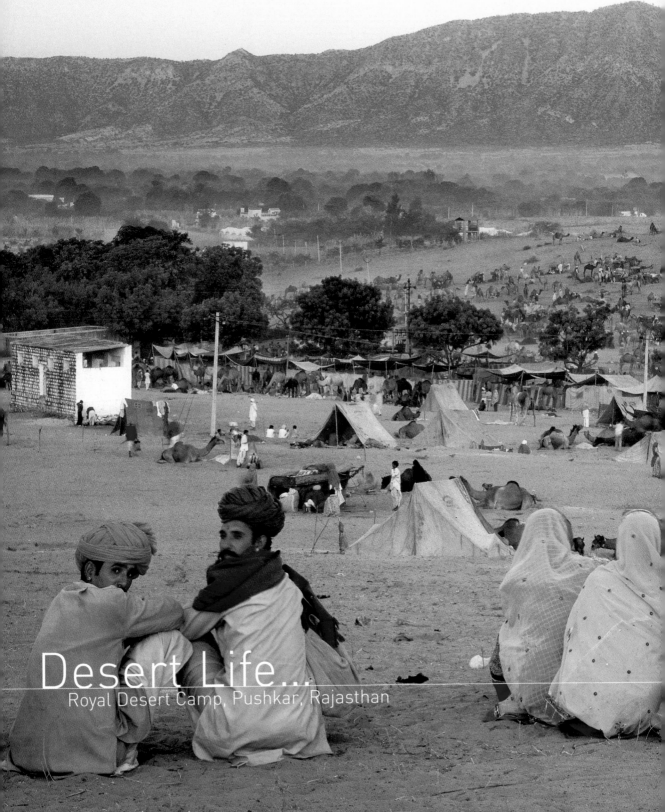

Desert Life...
Royal Desert Camp, Pushkar, Rajasthan

Desert Life

When at the start of the seventeenth century, the Indian ruler Jahangir embarked on a pleasure trip to Kashmir, he was a bit worried that the palaces there would not be up to his standards. He decided to travel with a complete entourage and his own tent city – and resided in luxurious marquees with soft beds and pillows, beautiful carpets and fabrics, sparkling glass and porcelain, a mobile kitchen and evening entertainment. The "Royal Desert Camp" was invented and from then on became a fixed part of the nobility's family parties, hunting excursions or wedding celebrations. In the meantime, normal mortals also get the chance to camp in royal style – at the Pushkar Fair, the most colourful and perhaps most beautiful event that Rajastan has to offer. To refer to it as a "folklore show" would almost be an insult – the Pushkar Fair is the largest camel trade fair in the world. It is also a place of pilgrimage for the Hindus, who wash away all their worries in the holy waters of the Pushkar Lake; a fashion show where India's women show themselves at their most beautiful and where they even newly dress and perfume the camels. In short, the Pushkar Fair is the distillation of tradition and joie de vivre for an entire region.

Book to pack: "A Son of the Circus" by John Irving

Royal Desert Camp
c/o Jagat Place
Pushkar – 305022
District Ajmer, Rajasthan, India
Tel. + 91 (145) 277 20 01 and 277 24 01
Fax + 91 (145) 277 22 26
Email: hotel_pushkar_palace@hotmail.com;
hppalace@datainfosys.net
Website: www.hotelpushkarpalace.com
www.great-escapes-hotels.com

DIRECTIONS	Pushkar is situated in the desert between Jodhpur and Jaipur, 140 km / 225 miles east of Jaipur Airport. Nearest train station is Ajmer (13 km / 8 miles).
RATES	$$
TENTS	234 comfortable tents with connected bathrooms (running water, toilet), beds, fan heater.
FOOD	Restaurant tent with specialties from India and Rajasthan, coffee shop.
HISTORY	Every November at the Pushkar Fair, the seventeenth century notion of the tent-city springs back to life.
X-FACTOR	The most luxurious camp site in the world.

Die Wüste lebt

Als der indische Herrscher Jahangir zu Beginn des 17. Jahrhunderts eine Vergnügungsfahrt nach Kaschmir unternahm, war er etwas in Sorge, dass die dortigen Paläste seinen Ansprüchen nicht genügen könnten. Er beschloss daher, mit kompletter Entourage und seiner eigenen Zeltstadt zu reisen – und residierte unter Luxusplanen mit weichen Betten und Kissen, traumhaften Teppichen und Stoffen, blinkendem Glas und Porzellan, einer mobile Küche und abendlichem Entertainment. Das »Royal Desert Camp« war erfunden und wurde fortan zum festen Bestandteil von adligen Familienfesten, Jagdausflügen oder Hochzeitspartys des Adels. Inzwischen haben auch Normalsterbliche die Möglichkeit, königlich zu campen – anlässlich der Pushkar Fair, dem farbenprächtigsten und vielleicht schönsten Event, das Rajasthan zu bieten hat. Es mit dem Begriff »Folkloreshow« zu umschreiben, wäre fast eine Beleidigung – die Pushkar Fair ist die größte Kamelmesse der Welt, eine Pilgerstätte für die Hindus, die in den heiligen Wassern des Pushkar Lake die Sorgen ihres ganzen Lebens wegwaschen, eine Modenschau, bei der sich Indiens Frauen von ihrer schönsten Seite zeigen und sogar die Kamele neu eingekleidet und parfümiert werden, kurz: die Pushkar Fair ist das Destillat der Traditionen und der Lebensfreude einer ganzen Region.

Buchtipp: »Zirkuskind« von John Irving

La vie du désert

Alors qu'il était sur le point d'entreprendre, au début du 17e siècle, un voyage d'agrément au Cachemire, le seigneur indien Jahangir se demanda soudain si les palais de cette région lui offriraient le confort auquel il était habitué. Il décida donc d'installer, pour lui et sa cour, un véritable campement. C'est ainsi que le prince résida dans des tentes somptueuses équipées de lits et de coussins moelleux, de tapis et d'étoffes de rêves, de porcelaines et de verres étincelants, d'une cuisine roulante, et permettant d'organiser le soir les divertissements les plus splendides. Le « Royal Desert Camp » était né et la noblesse du pays s'accoutuma bien vite à ce mode de résidence pour ses fêtes de famille, ses parties de chasse et ses mariages. Aujourd'hui, le commun des mortels a lui aussi la possibilité de camper comme un seigneur indien – et ce, à l'occasion de la foire de Pushkar, l'une des manifestations les plus colorées et peut-être les plus belles qui se déroulent au Rajasthan. La décrire comme un « spectacle folklorique » serait presque lui faire injure. La foire de Pushkar est la plus grande foire aux chameaux du monde et un lieu de pèlerinage pour les Hindous qui viennent se laver de leurs péchés dans les eaux du lac Pushkar. Mais elle est aussi un défilé de mode où les femmes indiennes se présentent parées de leurs plus beaux atours et où l'on habille même de neuf les chameaux que l'on a parfumés. En bref, la foire de Pushkar est un condensé des traditions et de la joie de vivre de toute une région.

Livre à emporter : « Un enfant de la balle » de John Irving

ANREISE	Pushkar liegt in der Wüste zwischen Jodhpur und Jaipur, 140 km östlich des Flughafens Jaipur. Nächster Bahnhof ist Ajmer (13 km).
PREIS	$$
ZELTE	234 komfortable Zelte mit angeschlossenem Bad (fließendes Wasser, Toilette), Betten, Heizlüfter.
KÜCHE	Restaurantzelt mit Spezialitäten aus Indien und Rajasthan, Coffee Shop.
GESCHICHTE	Die Idee der Zeltstadt aus dem 17. Jahrhundert lebt jedes Jahr im November bei der Pushkar Fair neu auf.
X-FAKTOR	Der luxuriöseste Campingplatz der Welt.

ACCÈS	Situé dans le désert entre Jodhpur et Jaipur, à 140 km à l'est de l'aéroport de Jaipur et à 13 km de la gare d'Ajmer.
PRIX	$$
TENTES	234 tentes confortables avec salle de bains attenante (eau courante, toilettes), lits, chauffage électrique.
RESTAURATION	Tente-restaurant proposant des spécialités de l'Inde et du Rajasthan, Coffee Shop.
HISTOIRE	L'idée de campement née au 17e siècle revit chaque année en novembre pendant la foire de Pushkar.
LE « PETIT PLUS »	Le camping le plus luxueux du monde.

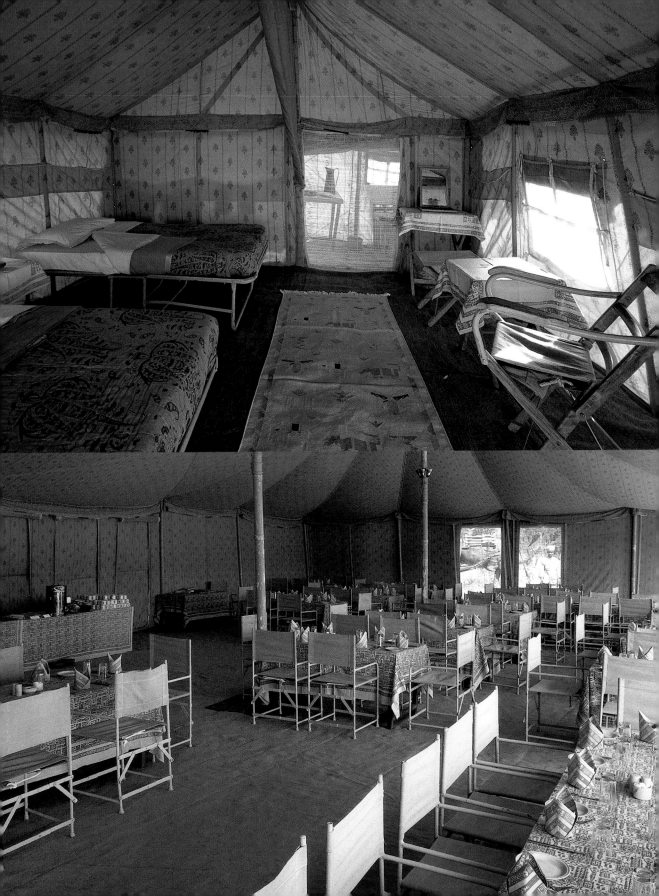

Living in a Fairytale...
Narain Niwas Palace, Jaipur, Rajasthan

Living in a Fairytale

Amar Singh Ji was one of the most influential men in Rajasthan during the early twentieth century. He was Thakur of Kanota, General of the Jaipur Armed Forces and close confidant of the Maharaja. A 24-hour job, one might think – but despite all of his responsibilities Amar Singh Ji still had time for his most important hobby: keeping a journal. He recorded his life on several thousand pages and also told of the construction of his country estate, which he had built in 1928 and which was named after his father Narain, former police chief of Jaipur. He spent his free time at his desk in this house, walking through the park or riding in the nearby jungle to shoot birds, wild pigs and even the occasional panther. Today the estate has been turned into a beautiful and relatively unknown palace hotel in which the Anglo-Indian style of the Victorian era lives on. While the exterior is cream coloured, strong yellow and ochre tones prevail inside, from the antique furnishings to the dashes of colour here and there – from a colourful pane of glass to a painted archway. And even if the leisure activities are not as exciting as they were during the times of the passionate hunter Amar Singh Ji, in the mango garden or at the pool one does experience the typical atmosphere and hospitality of ancient Rajasthan.

Book to pack: "May You Be the Mother of a Hundred Sons: A Journey Among the Women of India" by Elisabeth Bumiller

Narain Niwas Palace
Kanota Bagh, Narain Singh Road
Jaipur – 302004, Rajasthan, India
Tel. +91 (141) 256 12 91
Fax +91 (141) 256 10 45
Email: info@hotelnarainniwas.com
Website: www.hotelnarainniwas.com
www.great-escapes-hotels.com

DIRECTIONS	Situated in the centre of Jaipur, 11 km/7 miles from the airport and 5 km/3 miles from the train station.
RATES	$
ROOMS	24 standard rooms, 7 suites.
FOOD	Indian and Chinese specialties as well as western menus.
HISTORY	Built in 1928 as the Thakur's country estate, later converted to a hotel.
X-FACTOR	Luxurious country estate – and right in the middle of the city.

Wohnen wie im Märchen

Amar Singh Ji war einer der einflussreichsten Männer im Rajasthan des frühen 20. Jahrhunderts – Thakur von Kanota, General der Streitkräfte von Jaipur und enger Vertrauter des Maharadschas. Ein 24-Stunden-Job, so könnte man meinen, doch Amar Singh Ji hatte trotz all seiner Verpflichtungen Zeit für sein wichtigstes Hobby, das Tagebuchschreiben. Auf mehreren tausend Seiten hielt er sein Leben fest und erzählte auch vom Bau seines Landsitzes, den er anno 1928 errichten und nach seinem Vater Narain, einst der Polizeichef von Jaipur, benennen ließ. In diesem Haus saß er in seiner Freizeit am Schreibtisch, spazierte durch den Park oder ritt in den nahen Dschungel, um einen Vogel, ein Wildschwein oder vielleicht sogar einen Panther zu schießen. Heute ist aus dem Anwesen ein schönes und vergleichsweise unbekanntes Palasthotel geworden, in dem der angloindische Stil der viktorianischen Ära fortlebt. Außen cremefarben wird Narain Niwas innen von kräftigen Gelb- und Ockertönen beherrscht, von antikem Mobiliar und dem ein oder anderen Farbtupfer – sei es eine bunte Glasscheibe oder ein bemalter Torbogen. Und sind auch die Freizeitaktivitäten nicht mehr ganz so aufregend wie zu Zeiten des passionierten Jägers Amar Singh Ji, so erlebt man im Mangogarten oder am Pool doch die typische Atmosphäre und Gastfreundschaft des alten Rajasthan.

Buchtipp: »Hundert Söhne sollst Du haben. Frauenleben in Indien« von Elisabeth Bumiller

Habiter un palais de conte de fées

Amar Singh Ji, qui fut thakur de Kanota, général des armées de Jaipur et intime du maharadjah, a été l'un des hommes les plus influents du Rajasthan au début du 20e siècle. Malgré cet emploi du temps chargé, Amar Singh Ji réussissait à trouver des moments libres pour s'adonner à son occupation favorite, écrire son journal. Sur plusieurs milliers de pages, il a noté ses faits et gestes quotidiens et raconte aussi la construction de la résidence de campagne qu'il fit réaliser en 1928 et nommer d'après son père Narain, ex-chef de la police de Jaipur.

C'est ici qu'il passait ses loisirs à écrire, à se promener dans le parc ou à se rendre à cheval dans la jungle toute proche pour chasser un oiseau, un sanglier, peut-être même une panthère. Aujourd'hui, la propriété est devenue un hôtel superbe et relativement peu connu dans lequel le style anglo-indien de l'ère victorienne continue de déployer son élégance teintée d'exotisme.

Derrière une façade couleur crème, Narain Niwas est dominé à l'intérieur par des tons jaune vif et ocre, un mobilier ancien et, ici et là, un accent de couleur vive, une vitre multicolore ou une arcade peinte, par exemple. Et si les activités proposées ne sont plus aussi excitantes que du temps du chasseur passionné Amar Singh Ji, l'hôte qui se promène dans le jardin planté de manguiers ou se détend près de la piscine fait l'expérience de l'atmosphère caractéristique et de la convivialité de l'ancien Rajasthan.

Livre à emporter : « Compartiment pour dames » d'Anita Nair

ANREISE	Im Zentrum von Jaipur gelegen, 11 km vom Flughafen und 5 km vom Bahnhof entfernt.
PREIS	$
ZIMMER	24 Standardzimmer, 7 Suiten.
KÜCHE	Indische und chinesische Spezialitäten, außerdem westliche Menüs.
GESCHICHTE	1928 als Landsitz des Thakurs erbaut, später zum Hotel umgebaut.
X-FAKTOR	Luxuriöses Landhaus – und das mitten in der Stadt.

ACCÈS	Situé au centre de Jaipur, à 11 km de l'aéroport et à 5 km de la gare.
PRIX	$
CHAMBRES	24 chambres standard, 7 suites.
RESTAURATION	Spécialités indiennes et chinoises, menus occidentaux.
HISTOIRE	Construit en 1928 pour servir de maison de campagne au thakur, transformé plus tard en hôtel.
LE « PETIT PLUS »	Une luxueuse maison de campagne – au cœur de la ville.

A Giant Treasure Chest...

Samode Palace, Jaipur, Rajasthan

A Giant Treasure Chest
My palace, my panorama: As a guest in the legendary
Samode Palace you have an excellent opportunity to live
like a king. The sandstone-coloured hotel stands like an
immense fortress at the foot of the Aravalli Range, the
mountain chain which dominates northwest India. When
you walk through the gateway, you are greeted by an over-
sized treasure chest adorned with marble from nearby
quarries; dark wood and sparkling glass; delicately orna-
mented pillars and traditional carpets. The mosaics, which
fill entire walls, are so vast that it would take more than a
lifetime to count the number of tiny stones and the hours
of work that went into them. It is pure splendour – yet does
not overawe because the designers of this masterpiece have
managed to create space and distance, to combine light and
harmonious colours, and to rely completely on symmetry.
The ancient architecture and handcrafted art of Rajasthan
are also continued through the rooms. Anyone wishing to
extend this trip through time, can just mount a horse or
camel and ride through the village of Samode to stop for
lunch under the mango trees.
My palace, my panorama – and my picnic.
Book to pack: "A Fine Balance" by Rohinton Mistry

Samode Palace
Gangapole, Jaipur
Rajasthan – 302002, India
Tel. +91 (141) 263 24 07
Fax +91 (141) 263 13 97
Email: reservations@samode.com
Website: www.samode.com
www.great-escapes-hotels.com

DIRECTIONS	Situated 250 km/155 miles northwest of Delhi Airport, 56 km/35 miles from Jaipur Airport (transfers upon request).
RATES	$$$
ROOMS	25 deluxe rooms, 15 deluxe suites, 3 royal suites.
FOOD	Traditional specialties from Rajasthan.
HISTORY	A former Rajput fort and luxury hotel since 1987.
X-FACTOR	Even the pool is decorated with marble and mosaics.

Eine Schatztruhe von Format

Mein Palast, mein Panorama: Im legendären Samode Palace
hat der Traum vom Gast als König die besten Chancen, Wirklichkeit zu werden. Wie eine mächtige Festung liegt das
sandsteinfarbene Hotel am Fuß der Aravalli Range, der
Gebirgskette, die den Nordwesten Indiens beherrscht. Wer
durchs Tor tritt, dem öffnet sich eine überdimensionale
Schatztruhe. Mit Marmor aus den nahen Steinbrüchen,
dunklem Holz und funkelndem Glas, mit filigran verzier-
ten Bögen, traditionellen Teppichen und raumhohen Mosa-
iken, bei denen ein Leben nicht ausreichen würde, um die
Anzahl der Steinchen und der aufgewendeten Arbeitsstun-
den zu zählen. Es ist Pracht pur – und dass sie einen nicht
sofort erschlägt, liegt daran, dass man im Samode Palace das
Kunststück fertiggebracht hat, Raum und Weite zu schaffen,
helle und harmonische Farben zu kombinieren und ganz
auf Symmetrie zu setzen. Die alte Architektur und Handwerkskunst Rajasthans sind auch in den Zimmern präsent –
wer die Zeitreise noch weiter fortsetzen möchte, reitet hoch
zu Pferd oder zu Kamel durch das Dorf Samode und legt
anschließend eine Lunch-Pause unter Mangobäumen ein.
Mein Palast, mein Panorama – und mein Picknick.
Buchtipp: »Das Gleichgewicht der Welt« von Rohinton Mistry

Un univers fabuleux

Mon palais, mon panorama : la devise « le client est roi » a
toutes les chances de se réaliser dans le légendaire Samode
Palace. Telle une imposante forteresse, l'hôtel de couleur
grès est situé au pied des monts Aravalli, une chaîne monta-
gneuse qui domine le nord-ouest de l'Inde. Celui qui pousse
le portail, se retrouve subitement dans un univers fabuleux.
Marbre provenant des carrières toutes proches, boiseries fon-
cées et cristal étincelant, arcades travaillées de façon filigrane, tapis traditionnels et mosaïques couvrant les murs jusqu'au plafond – une vie entière ne suffirait pas à compter
toutes les petites pierres et les heures de travail. La splendeur à l'état pur – et si elle n'étourdit pas le client c'est parce
qu'au Samode Palace on est parvenu à susciter une sensation d'espace et de lointain, à marier les couleurs claires et
harmonieuses et à créer de la symétrie. L'architecture et
l'artisanat traditionnels sont également présents dans les
chambres. Celui qui désire poursuivre son voyage dans le
temps, fera une promenade à cheval ou à dos de chameau
à travers le village de Samode, promenade qu'il interrompra
à midi pour un lunch à l'ombre des manguiers. Mon palais,
mon panorama – et mon pique-nique.
Livre à emporter : « L'Equilibre du monde » de Rohinton Mistry

ANREISE	250 km nordwestlich vom Flughafen Delhi gelegen, 56 km vom Flughafen Jaipur entfernt (Transfers auf Wunsch).
PREIS	$$$
ZIMMER	25 Deluxe-Zimmer, 15 Deluxe-Suiten, 3 Royal-Suiten.
KÜCHE	Traditionelle Spezialitäten aus Rajasthan.
GESCHICHTE	Ursprünglich eine Festung der Rajputen, seit 1987 ein Luxushotel.
X-FAKTOR	Ein indisches Gesamtkunstwerk. Sogar der Pool ist mit Marmor und Mosaiken verziert.

ACCÈS	A 250 km au nord-ouest de l'aéroport de Delhi et à 56 km de l'aéroport de Jaipur (transfert sur demande).
PRIX	$$$
CHAMBRES	25 chambres de luxe, 15 suites de luxe, 3 suites royales.
RESTAURATION	Spécialités traditionnelles du Rajasthan.
HISTOIRE	A l'origine petite forteresse des Rajput, ouvert en 1987 comme hôtel de luxe.
LE « PETIT PLUS »	Même la piscine est en marbre et en mosaïque.

Gone Hunting...

Sardar Samand Palace, Jodhpur, Rajasthan

Gone Hunting

The Maharaja did not think much of huge palaces with thousands of turrets and arcades. He was a down-to-earth type of person; he liked nature and hunting – and Art Deco. In 1933, Umaid Singh had a weekend residence built in a style quite unique in India. His lodge reigns high above an artificial lake whose water is speckled pink with flamingos; its grey-brown stone seems to have merged with the surrounding rock, and it sports a kind of lookout tower with a white domed roof and turquoise-coloured balustrades. Inside one is amazed at the number of ways that sage green and salmon pink can be combined and at how successful the Maharaja was at hunting. A gazelle peers out from the wall; a buffalo watches over the door; a hollowed horn serves as an ashtray; books are stacked on elephant feet that are covered in leopard skin. Much of the decor also carries the trademark of Polish artist Stefan Norblin, who gave the Sardar Samand a complete facelift in the 1940s, turning it into an eccentric but extremely amusing lady. Not much has changed since; the descendents of the Maharaja only allow for small repairs if the original building material is preserved. The hotel comprises only 19 rooms; the owners themselves live in the others – because even today, the family still does not think much of huge palaces with thousands of turrets and arcades.

Book to pack: "Freedom at Midnight" by Larry Collins & Dominique Lapierre

Sardar Samand Palace
Sardar Samand, District Pali
Jodhpur – 306103
Rajasthan, India
Tel. +91 (2960) 245001-3
Fax +91 (0291) 2571240
Email: holidays@welcomheritagehotels.com
Website: www.welcomheritagehotels.com
www.great-escapes-hotels.com

DIRECTIONS	Situated 60 km/37 miles southeast of Jodhpur Airport, on the shore of Sardar Samand Lake.
RATES	$
ROOMS	19 deluxe rooms in Art-Deco style.
FOOD	Restaurant with specialities from India and Rajasthan as well as continental cuisine.
HISTORY	Built in 1933 as a hunting lodge; enlarged and renovated in the 1940s.
X-FACTOR	Highly unusual – but very agreeable.

Auf der Jagd

Von riesigen Palästen mit tausenden von Türmchen und Arkaden hielt der Maharadscha nicht viel. Er war ein bodenständiger Typ, mochte die Natur und die Jagd – und Art déco. 1933 ließ Umaid Singh eine Wochenendresidenz bauen, deren Stil in Indien wohl einmalig ist. Hoch über einem Stausee mit von Flamingos rosa gesprenkeltem Wasser thront eine Lodge, deren grau-brauner Stein mit dem Fels verwachsen scheint und die eine Art Aussichtsturm mit weißem Kuppeldach und türkisfarbene Balustraden besitzt. Im Inneren staunt man, auf wie viele Arten sich Schilfgrün und Lachsfarben kombinieren lassen – und wie viel Erfolg der Maharadscha beim Jagen hatte. Hier schaut eine Gemse aus der Wand, dort bewacht ein Büffel die Tür; Zigarettenasche landet in ausgehöhltem Horn, Bücher stapeln sich auf mit Leopardenfell bezogenen Elefantenfüßen. Vieles trägt auch die Handschrift des polnischen Künstlers Stefan Norblin, der Sardar Samand in den vierziger Jahren einem Facelifting unterzog und es zu einer exzentrischen, aber ungeheuer amüsanten Lady machte. Seitdem hat sich hier nicht mehr viel verändert; die Nachfahren des Maharadschas erlauben selbst kleine Reparaturen nur dann, wenn die ursprüngliche Bausubstanz erhalten bleibt. Als Hotel dienen übrigens nur 19 Zimmer. In den anderen Räumen wohnen die Eigentümer selbst – denn von riesigen Palästen mit tausenden von Türmchen und Arkaden hält die Familie auch heute noch nicht viel.

**Buchtipp: »Gandhi.Um Mitternacht die Freiheit«
von Larry Collins und Dominique Lapierre**

Les plaisirs de la chasse

Le maharadjah n'affectionnait guère les palais aux multiples tours et arcades. Homme aux goûts simples, il aimait la chasse et la nature – ainsi que l'art Déco. En 1933, Umaid Singh se fit construire une résidence secondaire dont le style est certainement unique en Inde. Dominant un barrage dont les eaux sont colorées ici et là par les flamants roses, le bâtiment a été construit avec des pierres d'un gris brunâtre qui semblent se fondre avec la falaise. Il se distingue surtout par sa tour coiffée d'une coupole blanche et par ses balustrades turquoises. A l'intérieur, les multiples combinaisons de vert et de saumon ainsi que les nombreux trophées de chasse du maharadjah attirent le regard. Ici, une gazelle nous observe accrochée au mur, là un buffle garde la porte. Les cendres de cigarette sont déposées dans une corne évidée et les livres s'empilent sur des pieds d'éléphant recouverts d'une peau de léopard. Beaucoup de choses portent aussi la signature de l'artiste polonais Stefan Norblin qui, dans les années quarante, fit subir un lifting à Sardar Samand le transformant ainsi en lady excentrique mais incroyablement amusante. Depuis cette époque, rien n'a changé ou presque. Même pour les petites réparations, les héritiers du maharadjah veillent à ce que la substance du bâtiment ne soit pas modifiée. D'ailleurs l'hôtel ne compte que 19 chambres, les autres pièces sont occupées par les propriétaires – aujourd'hui encore la famille n'affectionne guère les palais aux multiples tours et arcades.

Livre à emporter : « Cette nuit la liberté » de Larry Collins et Dominique Lapierre

ANREISE	60 km südöstlich vom Flughafen Jodhpur gelegen, am Ufer des Sardar Samand Lake.	ACCÈS	Situé à 60 km au sud-est de l'aéroport de Jodhpur, sur les rives du lac Sardar Samand.
PREIS	$	PRIX	$
ZIMMER	19 Deluxe-Zimmer im Art-déco-Stil.	CHAMBRES	19 chambres de luxe décorées dans le style art Déco.
KÜCHE	Restaurant mit Spezialitäten aus Indien und Rajasthan, außerdem kontinentale Küche.	RESTAURATION	Restaurant proposant des spécialités indiennes et du Rajasthan, ainsi qu'une cuisine continentale.
GESCHICHTE	1933 als Jagdhaus erbaut, in den vierziger Jahren erweitert und renoviert.	HISTOIRE	Construit en 1933 comme pavillon de chasse, agrandi et rénové dans les années quarante.
X-FAKTOR	Ganz schön schräg – aber sehr sympathisch.	LE « PETIT PLUS »	Plutôt bizarre – mais très sympathique.

On Her Majesty's Secret Serv

Devi Garh, Udaipur, Rajasthan

On Her Majesty's Secret Service

If a James Bond film director ever needed another setting in India – one where, on behalf of her majesty, 007 could hurl black-clad figures over walls and be seduced by long-legged women – then there would be no better place than Devi Garh. Both fascinating and awe-inspiring, the fort lords over the Aravalli Range near Udaipur; surrounded by mountains on three sides and a blue-grey velvet sky above. Its history really is something for the movies: Sajja Singh was given the building as thanks for his services and loyalty in the Battle of Haldighati (1576) when Maharana Pratap fought against the Mogul emperor Akbar. The palace presides over one of the three entrances to the valley of Udaipur and since being transformed into a luxury hotel is one of Rajasthan's most attractive addresses. Here, what you find beneath splendid archways and in the high halls, is more what you would expect of a loft residence in a big city: clear forms and colours, minimalist and functional design, marble and metal. Devi Garh reflects Asia's puristic side – which brings so much in terms of aesthetics and atmosphere, so much splendour and glamour, that it almost seems too beautiful to be real. A genuinely cinematic setting.

Book to pack: "The Sleeping Tiger" by Shashi Deshpande

Devi Garh
Delwara, NH8, Near Eklingji, Nathdwara
District Rajsamand, 313202
Rajasthan, India
Tel. +91 (2953) 28 92 11
Fax +91 (2953) 28 93 57
Email: devigarh@deviresorts.com
Website: www.deviresorts.com
www.great-escapes-hotels.com

DIRECTIONS	Situated 26 km/16 miles northeast of Udaipur (domestic flights from Delhi or Mumbai).
RATES	$$$
ROOMS	23 individually furnished suites. From October to March, 6 tents are also available.
FOOD	Innovative Asian cuisine based on the elaboration of traditional recipes. In addition, continental menus.
HISTORY	Built at the end of the sixteenth century. Following a 10-year period of renovation, it has been a luxury hotel since 2000.
X-FACTOR	One of the most beautiful Design Hotels in Asia.

Im Auftrag Ihrer Majestät

Sollte ein Regisseur von James Bond jemals wieder eine
Kulisse in Indien suchen, vor der 007 im Auftrag Ihrer
Majestät schwarz vermummte Gestalten über Mauern wer-
fen und langbeinigen Frauen zum Opfer fallen kann – es
gäbe keinen besseren Platz als Devi Garh. Faszinierend und
Furcht einflößend zugleich thront das Fort in der Aravalli
Range bei Udaipur; an drei Seiten von Bergen umgeben und
über sich einen Himmel wie aus blaugrauem Samt. Seine
Geschichte ist durchaus kinotauglich: Sajja Singh erhielt die
Trutzburg als Dank für seine Verdienste und Loyalität in der
Schlacht von Haldighati (1576), als Maharana Pratap gegen
den Mogulkaiser Akbar kämpfte. Seitdem beherrscht der
Palast einen der drei Eingänge ins Tal von Udaipur und
gehört nach seiner Verwandlung in ein Luxushotel zu den
attraktivsten Adressen Rajasthans. Was hier unter prachtvollen Torbögen und in hohen Hallen zu sehen ist, würde man
sonst eher in einem Großstadtloft erwarten: klare Formen
und Farben, minimalistisches und funktionales Design,
Marmor und Metall. Devi Garh zeigt Asiens puristische
Seite – und gewinnt genau dadurch so viel Ästhetik und
Atmosphäre, so viel Glanz und Glamour, dass es beinahe
unwirklich schön wirkt. Eine echte Kinokulisse eben.
Buchtipp: »Der schlafende Tiger« von Shashi Deshpande

Entre tradition et modernité

Si jamais un réalisateur voulait tourner un nouveau James
Bond en Inde et cherchait un endroit où l'agent secret pourrait jeter des hommes emmitouflés de voiles noirs en bas
des murailles et se laisser séduire par de ravissantes créa-
tures – Devi Garh serait le cadre idéal.
A la fois fascinant et inquiétant, le fort trône au milieu des
collines d'Aravali près d'Udaipur. Les montagnes l'enserrent
sur trois côtés, un ciel de velours bleu gris le surplombe.
Son histoire est de l'étoffe dont on fait les films à succès :
Sajja Singh reçut la forteresse en récompense de ses bons
et loyaux services à la bataille de Haldighati (1576), quand
Maharana Pratap affrontait l'empereur mogol Akbar.
Depuis cette époque, le palais domine l'un des trois accès à
la vallée d'Udaipur et, depuis sa transformation en hôtel de
luxe, il est l'une des adresses les plus fameuses du Rajasthan
– et des plus surprenantes : les formes et les couleurs nettes
et claires, le design minimaliste et fonctionnel, le marbre et
le métal que l'on peut voir ici sous les superbes arcades et
dans les hautes salles, semblent échappés d'un loft de la
métropole.
Devi Garh nous présente le côté puriste de l'Asie et acquiert
ainsi tant de grâce harmonieuse et d'atmosphère, tant d'éclat
et de glamour, qu'il semble d'une beauté quasi irréelle – un
vrai décor de cinéma.
**Livre à emporter : « La nuit retient ses fantômes »
de Shashi Deshpande**

ANREISE	26 km nordöstlich von Udaipur gelegen (Inlandsflüge ab Delhi oder Mumbai).
PREIS	$$$
ZIMMER	23 individuell ausgestattete Suiten. Von Oktober bis März stehen auch 6 Zelte zur Verfügung.
KÜCHE	Innovative asiatische Küche, für die traditionelle Rezepte verfeinert wurden. Außerdem kontinentale Menüs.
GESCHICHTE	Ende des 16. Jahrhunderts erbaut, nach zehnjähriger Renovierung seit 2000 ein Luxushotel.
X-FAKTOR	Prachtvoller Palast und eines der schönsten Designhotels Asiens.

ACCÈS	Situé à 26 km au nord-est d'Udaipur (vols intérieurs à partir de Delhi ou Mumbai).
PRIX	$$$
CHAMBRES	23 suites décorées de manière individuelle. 6 tentes disponibles d'octobre à mars.
RESTAURATION	Cuisine asiatique innovante avec plats traditionnels revisités. Menus continentaux.
HISTOIRE	Construit à la fin du 16ᵉ siècle. Ouvert en 2000 après dix ans de restauration.
LE « PETIT PLUS »	A la fois palais sublime et l'un des plus beaux hôtels design d'Asie.

The Maharaja's Jewel...

Udai Bilas Palace, Dungarpur, Rajasthan

Udai Bilas Palace, Dungarpur, Rajasthan

The Maharaja's Jewel

Dungarpur has long been known as the "city of the hills" – but Udai Singhji never really acquired a taste for the rocky landscape when he wanted to build a new palace in the mid-nineteenth century. Nevertheless, he was fascinated by Lake Gaibsagar and so he decided to build his own island with the region's pale pareva stones. The palace's first residential wing turned out to be relatively modest; then Udai Singhji put his whole love for architectural details into the "single-column palace", Ek Thambia Mahal, which overflows with turrets, arches, balustrades and marble inlay work and to-day still forms the heart of the complex. Later, the original owner's descendants clearly wanted to do something which would contrast the concise traditional design: They furnished the rooms added in 1940 entirely in the Art Deco style and decorated the awe-inspiring banquet hall with hunting trophies from the nearby forest. Since 2001 the hotel has also had a pool where the raised trunks of two white marble elephants spurt fountains of water. The tracks of real animals can be followed on the banks of the lake and in the nature reserve, since Dungarpur is considered an El Dorado for ornithologists and safari fans: leopards, antelopes and even flying squirrels can be seen here. And for any of you who do not feel that the plain offers enough attractions: Dungarpur's Juna Mahal, for instance, is one of the most splendid and oldest palaces of the region – it dates back to the thirteenth century.

Book to pack: "Ten Princes or the Dasha-kumara-charita" by Grazia Dandin

Udai Bilas Palace	
Dungarpur – 314001	
Rajasthan, India	
Tel. +91 (2964) 23 08 08	
Fax +91 (2964) 23 10 08	
Email: contact@udaibilaspalace.com	
Website: www.udaibilaspalace.com	
www.great-escapes-hotels.com	

DIRECTIONS	Situated at Lake Gaibsagar and at the edge of the nature reserve, 120 km/75 miles south of the airport at Udaipur.
RATES	$
ROOMS	10 rooms and 10 suites, all individually furnished in Art Deco style.
FOOD	Indian specialities; spiced more mildly than usual in consideration of western palates.
HISTORY	Built as a palace in the nineteenth century and extended in 1940.
X-FACTOR	A royal vacation just like on a private island.

Das Schmuckstück des Maharadschas

Seit jeher ist Dungarpur auch als »Stadt der Hügel« bekannt – doch mit dem felsigen Land konnte sich Udai Singhji nicht recht anfreunden, als er Mitte des 19. Jahrhunderts einen neuen Palast bauen wollte. Ihn faszinierte der Gaibsagar-See und hier schuf er aus dem hellen Pareva-Stein der Region seine eigene Insel. Der erste Wohnflügel fiel vergleichsweise bescheiden aus; Udai Singhji steckte seine ganze Liebe zu architektonischen Details in den »einsäuligen Palast« Ek Thambia Mahal, der von Türmchen, Bögen, Balustraden und Marmorintarsien nur so überquillt und noch heute das Herzstück des Komplexes ist. Dem geballten traditionellen Design wollten die Erben des einstigen Hausherrn offensichtlich einiges entgegensetzen: Sie richteten die 1940 angebauten Zimmer ganz im Art-déco-Stil ein und schmückten den Respekt einflößenden Bankettsaal mit Jagdtrophäen aus dem nahen Wald. Seit 2001 besitzt das Hotel auch einen Pool, in den zwei weiße Marmorelefanten aus erhobenen Rüsseln Wasserfontänen spritzen. Den Spuren echter Tiere kann man am Ufer des Sees und im Naturschutzgebiet folgen, denn Dungarpur gilt als Dorado für Ornithologen und Safarifans – hier werden regelmäßig Leoparden, Antilopen und sogar fliegende Eichhörnchen gesichtet. Und für alle, denen die Ebene noch nicht genug Attraktionen bietet, ist ebenfalls gesorgt: Mit dem Juna Mahal besitzt Dungarpur zum Beispiel einen der prachtvollsten und ältesten Paläste der Region – er stammt aus dem 13. Jahrhundert.

Buchtipp: »Krishnas Schatten« von Kiran Nagarkar

Le joyau du maharadjah

Depuis toujours Dungarpur est « la cité des collines », mais le maharawal Udai Singhji II ne la trouva pas à son goût quand il voulut construire un nouveau palais au milieu du 19e siècle. En revanche, il était fasciné par le lac Gaibsagar et fit d'abord élever juste au bord de celui-ci, en pierre bleu gris de Pareva locale, un pavillon modeste comparé à son autre palais : c'est que Udai Singhji II, grand amoureux de l'art et de l'architecture, consacra son énergie au « palais à une colonne » Ek Thambia Mahal qui offre une foule de tourelles, d'arcades, de balustrades et des frises en marbre sculpté, une merveille de l'architecture rajpoute, qui est resté le cœur du complexe.

Ses descendants ne partageaient manifestement pas sa prédilection pour le style traditionnel. Ils aménagèrent les chambres annexées en 1940 dans le plus pur style Art déco et décorèrent l'imposante salle de banquet avec des trophées de chasse – la jungle est toute proche. Depuis 2002, l'hôtel abrite aussi une piscine dans laquelle deux éléphants blancs en marbre font jaillir de l'eau de leur trompe fièrement dressée. On peut suivre les traces d'animaux sauvages sur les rives du lac et dans la réserve naturelle car Dungarpur est un véritable paradis pour les ornithologues et les amateurs de safaris. On y voit régulièrement des léopards, des antilopes et même des écureuils volants.

Et pour ceux à qui la plaine n'offre pas assez d'agréments – Dungarpur possède aussi le Juna Mahal, un des palais les plus splendides et les plus anciens de la région puisqu'il date du 13e siècle.

Livre à emporter : « Histoire des dix princes » de Grazia Dandin

ANREISE	Im Gaibsagar-See und am Rand eines Naturschutzgebietes gelegen, 120 km südlich des Flughafens von Udaipur.
PREIS	$
ZIMMER	10 Zimmer und 10 Suiten, alle individuell im Art-déco-Stil eingerichtet.
KÜCHE	Indische Spezialitäten – mit Rücksicht auf westliche Gaumen sanfter gewürzt als üblich.
GESCHICHTE	Mitte des 19. Jahrhunderts als Palast errichtet und 1940 ausgebaut.
X-FAKTOR	Königlicher Urlaub wie auf einer privaten Insel.

ACCÈS	Situé sur les rives du lac Gaibsagar et au bord d'une réserve naturelle. A 120 km au sud de l'aéroport d'Udaipur.
PRIX	$
CHAMBRES	10 chambres et 10 suites, toutes décorées individuellement dans le style Art déco.
RESTAURATION	Spécialités indiennes – moins épicées que ne le veut la coutume par égard pour les palais occidentaux.
HISTOIRE	Palais édifié au milieu du 19e siècle et agrandi en 1940.
LE « PETIT PLUS »	Des vacances royales.

On Cloud Nine...
Nilaya Hermitage, Goa

Nilaya Hermitage, Goa

On Cloud Nine

"Goa Dourada" is what the natives affectionately call it, "Golden Goa". And anyone who has lain even once on that famous beach – golden sand below, golden sun above – would agree with them. But this island on the west coast of India has an even broader palette of colours to offer – the most beautiful proof of which is the hotel Nilaya Hermitage. It opens up like a paintbox in the hills of Arpora with its bold and perfectly harmonised colours. Turquoise blue, yellow-green and bright orange are not generally considered to be the best of friends, but when you set eyes on them to-gether in the lobby of the Nilaya you become instantly con-vinced that exactly this combination is just perfection itself. With a lot of colour and typical accessories, Claudia Derain and Hari Ajwani have conjured a Portuguese flair into the rooms which recall Goa's colonial past. Also, thanks to the predomination of rounded forms in the design, one has the pleasant feeling that even the odd hard edge won't cause any problems. The rooms have been named after cosmic ele-ments like the sun, moon and fire – and the name "Nilaya" itself translates as nothing less than "heaven". By the way, many guests find their cloud nine by the pool, where east-meets-west specialties are served in the evenings.

Book to pack: "Voyage of Discovery" by Vasco da Gama

Nilaya Hermitage
Arpora Bhati
Goa 403518, India
Tel. +91 (832) 27 67 93
Fax +91 (832) 27 67 92
Email: info@nilaya.com
Website: www.nilaya.com
www.great-escapes-hotels.com

DIRECTIONS	Situated 350 km/217 miles south of Mumbai (the transfer from/to the airport is organized).
RATES	$$$
ROOMS	12 double rooms.
FOOD	Combines flavours from Goa, India, China and the Mediterranean area.
HISTORY	Opened in 1994 as an alternative to the classic beach resorts on Goa.
X-FACTOR	Multicultural vacation – Portugal meets India.

Auf Wolke sieben

»Goa Dourada« nennen es die Einheimischen liebevoll, »Goldenes Goa«. Und wer auch nur einmal an einem der berühmten Strände gelegen hat – goldenen Sand unter sich, die goldene Sonne über sich –, wird ihnen zustimmen. Doch die Insel an der Westküste Indiens hat noch eine breitere Farbpalette zu bieten – der hübscheste Beweis dafür ist das Hotel Nilaya Hermitage. In den Hügeln von Arpora öffnet es sich wie ein Malkasten mit mutigen, aber perfekt aufeinander abgestimmten Tönen. Türkisblau, Gelbgrün und leuchtendes Orange sind nicht immer die besten Freunde; doch wer sie in der Lobby des Nilaya sieht, ist innerhalb von Sekunden davon überzeugt, dass genau diese Kombination die einzig richtige und mögliche ist. Mit viel Farbe und typischen Accessoires zaubern Claudia Derain und Hari Ajwani auch in die Zimmer portugiesisches Flair und erinnern an die koloniale Vergangenheit Goas; und dank der überwiegend runden Formen hat man das gute Gefühl, sich auch an den wenigen echten Ecken gar nicht richtig stoßen zu können. Benannt sind die Räume nach kosmischen Elementen wie Sonne, Mond und Feuer – und »Nilaya« selbst bedeutet nichts Geringeres als »Himmel«. Wolke sieben ist für viele Gäste übrigens der Pool, an dem abends East-meets-West-Spezialitäten serviert werden.

**Buchtipp: »Die Entdeckung des Seewegs nach Indien«
von Vasco da Gama**

Le septième ciel

Les habitants l'appellent amoureusement « Goa Dourada », Goa la dorée. Et celui qui s'est déjà allongé sur l'une de ses célèbres plages, où l'or du sable joue avec l'or du soleil, ne pourra que partager ce sentiment. Pourtant l'île de la côte occidentale de l'Inde propose une gamme de couleurs encore plus vaste et le pkus bel exemple en est assurément l'hôtel Nilaya Hermitage. Dans les collines d'Arpora il se présente comme la palette d'un peintre, avec des coloris audacieux mais qui s'harmonisent entre eux. D'habitude le bleu turquoise, le vertjaune et l'orange vif ne font pas toujours bon ménage mais lorsqu'on les voit dans le hall de réception du Nilaya, on est tout de suite convaincu que cette combinaison de tons est la seule possible. En s'aidant de la couleur et d'accessoires typiques Claudia Derain et Hari Ajwani ont aussi donné aux chambres une atmosphère portugaise qui rappelle le passé colonial de Goa. Et grâce aux formes arrondies qui prédominent dans les pièces, il est possible de se déplacer librement sans craindre de se cogner à tout moment. Les chambres ont été baptisées d'après les éléments cosmiques, comme le soleil, la lune et le feu – et « Niyala » signifie le ciel. D'ailleurs pour beaucoup de clients le septième nuage est la piscine, au bord de laquelle des spécialités dites « East-meets-West » sont servies le soir.

**Livre à emporter : « La Découverte de la route des Indes »
de Vasco de Gama**

ANREISE	350 km südlich von Mumbai gelegen (Transfer ab/zum Flughafen wird organisiert).
PREIS	$$$
ZIMMER	12 Doppelzimmer.
KÜCHE	Verbindet Aromen aus Goa, Indien, China und dem Mittelmeerraum.
GESCHICHTE	1994 als Alternative zu den klassischen Strandresorts auf Goa eröffnet.
X-FAKTOR	Multikultureller Urlaub – hier liegt Portugal in Indien.

ACCÈS	Situé à 350 km au sud de Mumbai (le transfert entre l'aéroport et l'hôtel est organisé).
PRIX	$$$
CHAMBRES	12 chambres doubles.
RESTAURATION	Associe les arômes de Goa, de l'Inde, de la Chine et du bassin méditerranéen.
HISTOIRE	Ouvert en 1994 comme alternative aux hôtels de la plage classiques de Goa.
LE « PETIT PLUS »	Vacances multiculturelles – ici le Portugal se trouve en Inde.

Seeing Green...
Green Magic Nature Resort, Kerala

Green Magic Nature Resort, Kerala

Seeing Green

Those summers in the tree house were unique: Days spent in the woods behind my grandparents' house with my best friends and scratches on our legs, filled with secrets and giddiness and the nights spent between the sky and earth. Are these happy times all over and relegated to the past? No, these summers still exist: In the tropical rainforest of Kerala, three houses seem to sway in the treetops. They are suspended 25 meters above the ground and rather luxuriously equipped with a bedroom, a bathroom with shower and toilet, a covered veranda and outdoor seating. Hydraulic lifts, somewhat reminiscent of the cages used in mines, transport visitors and luggage right up into the heart of the jungle. What does the rustling of the foliage and the cries of the animals sound like? How does the light morning fog and the first rays of sun feel on one's skin? How fast is one's pulse during a thunderstorm or monsoon? Anyone preferring to experience the whims of nature with solid ground under their feet can move to one of the six eco-cottages instead. They too have been constructed by native craftsmen using only natural materials. Further proximity to nature is brought by walks along the Periyar Tiger Trail and even at mealtimes as well: Fruit and vegetables are from the resort's own farm and meals are prepared with the help of solar energy and served on banana leaves – this is the taste of Kerala.

Book to pack: "The Jungle Book" by Rudyard Kipling

Green Magic Nature Resort
c/o Tourindia
Post Box No. 163
Mahatma Gandhi Road
Trivandrum – 695001, Kerala, India
Tel. +91 (471) 233 04 37 and 233 15 07
Fax +91 (471) 233 14 07
Email: tourindia@vsnl.com
Website: www.tourindiakerala.com
www.great-escapes-hotels.com

DIRECTIONS	Situated 250 km/155 miles southwest of Bangalore, 65 km/40 miles from Calicut Airport.
RATES	$$
ROOMS	3 tree houses, 6 cottages.
FOOD	Local dishes consisting of fruit and vegetables (organic farming), served on banana leaves.
HISTORY	Eco-lodge that works together with the Kerala Forest Authority. In 1998 it received the International Environment Award.
X-FACTOR	Adventure holiday – right in the middle of the rainforest.

Alles im grünen Bereich

Diese Sommer im Baumhaus waren einzigartig. Damals, in Wäldchen hinter dem Haus der Großeltern – mit den besten Freunden und Schrammen an den Beinen, voller Geheimnisse und Schwindelgefühle und mit Nächten zwischen Himmel und Erde. Vorbei und zu Ende? Nein, diese Sommer gibt es noch: Im tropischen Regenwald von Kerala scheinen drei Häuser in den Baumkronen zu schweben. 25 Meter über dem Boden und geradezu luxuriös mit Schlafzimmer, Bad inklusive Dusche und Toilette, überdachter Veranda und Freisitz ausgestattet. Mit hydraulisch betriebenen Aufzügen, die ein bisschen an die Förderkörbe im Bergbau erinnern, kommen Bewohner und Gepäck nach oben, mitten ins Herz des Dschungels. Wie klingen das Rauschen der Blätter und die Schreie der Tiere? Wie fühlen sich der leichte Morgennebel und die ersten Sonnenstrahlen auf der Haut an? Wie schnell geht der Puls bei einem Gewitterregen oder Monsun? Wer die Launen der Natur lieber mit festem Boden unter den Füßen erlebt, kann in eines von sechs Eco-Cottages ziehen; sie sind ebenfalls mit natürlichen Materialien und von einheimischen Handwerkern gebaut. Auf Tuchfühlung mit der Natur geht man auch bei Wanderungen auf dem Periyar Tiger Trail und sogar beim Essen: Obst und Gemüse stammen aus eigenem Anbau, gekocht wird mit Hilfe von Solarenergie und serviert auf Bananenblättern – so schmeckt Kerala.

Buchtipp: »Das Dschungelbuch« von Rudyard Kipling

Dans la verdure

Ces étés étaient uniques. Avec mes meilleurs copains, nous avions construit une cabane perchée dans les arbres, dans le bois qui se trouvait derrière chez mes grands-parents – je me souviens des jambes toutes griffées, du trop-plein de secrets et de sentiments vertigineux et des nuits entre le ciel et la terre. On peut retrouver ces étés-là au Kerala, dans la forêt vierge, où trois cabanes semblent planer en haut des arbres. Elles se situent à 25 mètres au-dessus du sol et sont dotées de chambres à coucher, d'une salle de bains avec douche et d'un W.-C., d'une véranda couverte et d'un siège en plein air – le luxe. Dans des ascenseurs hydrauliques qui évoquent les cages des mineurs, les habitants et leurs bagages sont hissés dans la cime des arbres, au cœur de la jungle, en union directe avec la nature : écouter le bruissement des feuilles et les cris d'animaux ; sentir la légère brume matinale et les premiers rayons du soleil sur la peau ; trembler quand l'orage gronde et que la pluie se déverse sur le toit... Celui qui ne veut pas vivre à ce point dans l'intimité de la forêt peut s'installer dans un des six cottages, également construits avec des matériaux naturels par des artisans locaux. La nature n'est jamais loin lorsqu'on suit le Periyar Tiger Trail et même pendant les repas : les fruits et les légumes sont produits ici, ils sont cuits à l'aide de l'énergie solaire et servis sur des feuilles de bananier – c'est le goût du Kerala.

Livre à emporter : « Le livre de la jungle » de Rudyard Kipling

ANREISE	250 km südwestlich von Bangalore gelegen, 65 km vom Flughafen Calicut entfernt.
PREIS	$$
ZIMMER	3 Baumhäuser, 6 Cottages.
KÜCHE	Einheimische Gerichte aus Obst und Gemüse (biologischer Anbau), serviert auf Bananenblättern.
GESCHICHTE	Eco-Lodge, die mit der Kerala Forest Authority zusammenarbeit. 1998 mit dem International Environment Award ausgezeichnet.
X-FAKTOR	Abenteuerurlaub – mitten im Regenwald.

ACCÈS	Situé à 250 km au sud-ouest de Bangalore, à 65 km de l'aéroport de Calicut.
PRIX	$$
CHAMBRES	3 cabanes, 6 cottages.
RESTAURATION	Plats régionaux à base de fruits et de légumes (agriculture biologique), servis sur des feuilles de bananier.
HISTOIRE	Hôtel écologique qui collabore avec la Kerala Forest Authority. Le prix International Environment Award lui a été décerné en 1998.
LE « PETIT PLUS »	Les plaisirs de l'enfance au cœur de la forêt vierge.

The Enchanted Garden...
Shalimar Spice Garden Resort, Kerala

The Enchanted Garden

There is a simple remedy for the heat and humidity of the plains of Kerala: a trip to the mountains where, at the edge of the Periyar Tiger Reserve, the Shalimar Spice Garden Resort is located. At a height of 800 metres, where the air is relatively cool, the Italian Maria Angela Fernhof and the Indian Shaji Antony have created their own personal paradise and given it a name which is a combination of their own two first names. Life is simple up here, yet there also seems to be an excess of everything: The straw-covered cottages stand in the midst of bright green palm groves and amongst trees and plants where mangos, nutmeg and cardamom flourish – for hobby biologists, the tropical flora is even explained on small signs. The kitchen refines the Indian dishes by adding precisely the right amount of Italian flavouring (and vice versa). If after yoga and a massage in distant Europe or the United States, you wanted to wake up feeling as relaxed as you do here, it would require a lot of money and a lot of patience. Lovers of solitude will enjoy staying longer – everyone else should plan a safari in the nearby reserve and follow the tracks of wild elephants, leopards and deer.

Book to pack: "The God of Small Things" by Arundhati Roy

Shalimar Spice Garden Resort
Murikkady P.O. Kumily
Idukki District – 685535
Kerala, India
Tel. +91 (4869) 222 132
Fax +91 (4869) 22 3022
Email: reservations@anantara.in
Website: www.shalimarkerala.net
www.great-escapes-hotels.com

DIRECTIONS	Situated 150 km/93 miles southwest of Madurai Airport at the edge of the Periyar Tiger Reserve.
RATES	$$
ROOMS	7 cottages and 8 double rooms, all individually furnished.
FOOD	Indian-Italian dishes are served in the glass restaurant.
HISTORY	Constructed in 1996 as a comfortable resort which is close to nature and connects eastern and western elements.
X-FACTOR	A dream in an enchanted garden – a perfect hideaway.

Ein Haus im Grünen

Es gibt ein einfaches Rezept gegen die Hitze und Schwüle der Ebenen von Kerala: eine Fahrt in die Berge, wo am Rand des Periyar Tiger Reservats das Shalimar Spice Garden Resort steht. In 800 Metern Höhe und in vergleichsweise kühler Luft haben die Italienerin Maria Angela Fernhof und der Inder Shaji Antony ihr persönliches Paradies geschaffen und ihm einen aus ihren beiden Vornamen kombinierten Titel verliehen. Es ist ein einfaches Leben hier oben, das aber gleichzeitig alles im Überfluss zu haben scheint: Die strohgedeckten Cottages stehen inmitten leuchtend grüner Palmenhaine und unter Bäumen und Stauden, an denen Mango, Muskatnuss oder Kardamom gedeihen – für Hobby-biologen wird die Tropenflora sogar auf kleinen Schildern erklärt. Die Küche verfeinert indische Gerichte mit genau dem richtigen Hauch Italienaroma (und umgekehrt), und wollte man nach Yogastunden und Massagen im fernen Europa oder Amerika genauso entspannt aufstehen wie hier, man müsste viel Geld und Geduld aufbringen. Wer länger bleiben möchte, muss die Einsamkeit lieben – alle anderen sollten eine Safari im nahen Reservat planen und den Spuren wilder Elefanten, Leoparden und Hirsche folgen.
Buchtipp: »Der Gott der kleinen Dinge« von Arundhati Roy

Le jardin enchanté

Il existe une recette toute simple pour fuir la chaleur acca-blante de la vallée de Kerala : il suffit de se réfugier dans les montagnes où se trouve le Shalimar Spice Garden Resort, situé près de la réserve de tigres de Periyar. C'est ici, à 800 mètres d'altitude, là où l'air est plus frais, que l'Italienne Maria Angela Fernhof et l'Indien Shaji Antony ont créé leur petit paradis, qu'ils ont nommé en mariant leurs deux pré-noms. La vie dans ce lieu est à la fois simple et abondante. Les cottages aux toits recouverts de paille se trouvent au milieu d'une végétation éclatante d'arbres et d'arbustes ployant sous le poids des mangues et des noix de muscade. Cette flore tropicale est expliquée sur de petits panneaux à l'attention des biologistes amateurs. La cuisine combine avec bonheur les influences indiennes et italiennes des pro-priétaires, et il faudrait certainement débourser beaucoup d'argent en Amérique ou en Europe pour éprouver le même sentiment de détente après les massages ou les cours de yoga dispensés à l'hôtel. Le client qui désire prolonger son séjour doit aimer la solitude – sinon il a la possibilité de faire un safari dans la réserve toute proche où il pourra partir sur les traces des éléphants sauvages, des léopards et des cerfs.
Livre à emporter : « Le Dieu des petits riens » de Arundhati Roy

ANREISE	150 km südwestlich des Flughafens Madurai gelegen, am Rand des Periyar Tiger Reservats.
PREIS	$$
ZIMMER	7 Cottages und 8 Doppelzimmer, alle individuell einge-richtet.
KÜCHE	Im gläsernen Restaurant werden indisch-italienische Gerichte serviert.
GESCHICHTE	1996 als naturnahes und doch komfortables Resort erbaut, das östliche und westliche Elemente verbindet.
X-FAKTOR	Träumen im verwunschenen Garten – ein perfektes Hideaway.

ACCÈS	Situé à 150 km au sud-ouest de l'aéroport de Madurai, près de la réserve de tigres de Periyar.
PRIX	$$
CHAMBRES	7 cottages et 8 chambres doubles, tous aménagés de façon individuelle.
RESTAURATION	Cuisine italo-indienne servie dans le restaurant de verre.
HISTOIRE	Construit en 1996, l'hôtel à la fois proche de la nature et confortable, allie les éléments orientaux et occi-dentaux.
LE « PETIT PLUS »	Rêver dans un jardin enchanté – la retraite idéale.

The Journey is the Goal...
Houseboat, Kerala

Houseboat, Kerala

The Journey is the Goal

They look something like the scaly heads of reptiles, and when two of the boats swim towards one another and the helmsmen stir up the water with their long paddles, one thinks that a fight between two river dragons is about to break out. In comparison, life on board is very peaceful: Comfortably reclined in a deckchair, you let daily life on Kerala's shores pass by, doze in the shade of a sun roof made of palm leaves or sample the sharpness of the vegetable curry prepared by the onboard cook. "Kettuvallams" (rice boats) is the name for these long ships that traffic along Kerala's 1,500 kilometres of water – an extensive network of rivers, canals, lagoons and lakes, which comprises one of India's most enchanting landscapes. The boats are about 20 meters long and can be as wide as four meters. They have roofs made of bamboo poles, coconut fibres and palm leaves with numerous openings. They are furnished like small loggias with living spaces as well as a bathroom including a shower and toilet. They were formerly used to transport goods from one trading place to the next. Even today, postmen, campaigning politicians or missionaries use the kettuvallams to visit remote villages. But you need no special reason to board the ship as a tourist – on the boat, the journey is the goal.

Book to pack: "Nectar in a Sieve" by Kamala Markandaya

Houseboat, Kerala
c/o Tourindia
Post Box No. 163
Mahatma Gandhi Road
Trivandrum – 695001, Kerala, India
Tel. + 91 (471) 233 04 37 and 233 15 07
Fax + 91 (471) 233 14 07
Email: tourindia@vsnl.com
Website: www.tourindiakerala.com
www.great-escapes-hotels.com

DIRECTIONS	Tours are available, for example, starting at the Green Magic Nature Resort.
RATES	$$
ROOMS	Kettuvallams with one to three cabins (2 to 6 guests).
FOOD	Fresh fish and vegetable curries.
HISTORY	Backwater barges that are now houseboats for tourists.
X-FACTOR	A cruise with a difference that shows Kerala from a new perspective.

Der Weg ist das Ziel

Sie erinnern ein wenig an die schuppigen Köpfe von Reptilien; und wenn zwei der Boote aufeinanderzuschwimmen und die Steuermänner mit ihren langen Paddeln im Wasser herumrühren, erwartet man jeden Moment den Kampf zweier Flussdrachen. Dabei geht es an Bord so friedlich zu. Bequem im Deckchair zurückgelehnt lässt man den Alltag an Keralas Ufern an sich vorüberziehen, döst im Schatten eines Sonnendachs aus Palmwedeln oder testet die Schärfe des Gemüsecurrys, das der mitreisende Koch zubereitet hat. »Kettuvallams« (Reisboote) heißen die lang gezogenen Schiffe, die auf den 1500 Wasserkilometern von Kerala unterwegs sind – einem weit verzweigten Netz aus Flüssen, Kanälen, Lagunen und Seen, das eine der zauberhaftesten Landschaften Südindiens bildet. Um die zwanzig Meter lang und bis zu vier Meter breit sind die Boote, sie besitzen ein Dach aus Bambusstäben, Kokosfasern und Palmwedeln, das an mehreren Stellen geöffnet werden kann, und sind wie eine kleine Loggia mit Wohnräumen sowie einem Bad inklusive Dusche und Toilette ausgestattet. Früher transportierte man mit ihnen Waren von einem Handelsplatz zum nächsten, und noch heute sind Postboten, Politiker im Wahlkampf oder Missionare an Bord von Kettuvallams zu entlegenen Dörfern unterwegs. Wer sich als Tourist einschifft, braucht keine spezielle Aufgabe – auf dem Boot ist der Weg das Ziel.

Buchtipp: »Nektar in einem Sieb« von Kamala Markandaya

Au fil de l'eau

Les embarcations évoquent les têtes écailleuses de reptiles gigantesques, et lorsqu'elles s'avancent l'une vers l'autre, que les hommes fouillent l'eau de leurs longues perches, on s'attend à tout instant à voir s'affronter deux dragons aquatiques. Et dire que la vie est si paisible à bord. Confortablement installé dans une chaise longue sur le pont, on regarde défiler les rives du Kerala, on somnole sous un toit en feuilles de palmier ou on savoure un curry de légumes bien épicé préparé par le cuisinier du bord.

Les longues embarcations naviguent sur les 1500 kilomètres de cours d'eau du Kerala – un réseau dense de rivières, de canaux, de lagunes et de lacs qui forme l'un des paysages les plus enchanteurs du sud de l'Inde. Longs d'une vingtaine de mètres et jusqu'à quatre mètres de large, les « kettuvallam », ou bateaux à riz, ont un toit en bambou, en fibre de coco et en branches de palmier qui peut être ouvert à plusieurs endroits. Ils sont dotés, comme un petite loggia, de pièces à vivre, d'une salle de bains avec douche et de W.-C. Autrefois, les kettuvallam transportaient les marchandises d'une centre de commerce à l'autre et aujourd'hui encore les facteurs, les politiciens en campagne et les missionnaires les empruntent pour se rendre dans les villages isolés. Le touriste qui s'embarque ici le fait sans objectif précis – ici, le chemin est le but.

Livre à emporter : « Le riz et la mousson » de Kamala Markandaya

ANREISE	Angeboten werden Touren zum Beispiel ab dem Green Magic Nature Resort.
PREIS	$$
ZIMMER	Kettuvallams mit ein bis drei Kabinen (2 bis 6 Gäste).
KÜCHE	Frischer Fisch und Gemüsecurrys.
GESCHICHTE	Aus den ursprünglichen Transportbooten in den Backwaters von Südindien wurden Hausboote für Touristen.
X-FAKTOR	Die etwas andere Kreuzfahrt zeigt Kerala aus neuen Perspektiven.

ACCÈS	Choix de promenades, par exemple à partir du Green Magic Nature Resort.
PRIX	$$
CHAMBRES	Kettuvallam de 1 à 3 cabines (2 à 6 personnes).
RESTAURATION	Poisson frais et curry de légumes.
HISTOIRE	Les bateaux de transport circulant dans les back waters, ont été transformés en embarcations aménagées pour les touristes.
LE « PETIT PLUS »	Une croisière pour découvrir l'autre visage du Kerala.

The White House...
The Sun House, Galle

The Sun House, Galle

The White House

In Galle time seems to have stood still sometime during the colonial period. The slowly beating heart of the little city on Sri Lanka's south coast is a Dutch fort whose thick city walls conceal old merchants' houses and aged cars rattle through the narrow streets. It is where you can take evening strolls to Star Bastion and experience one of the kitschiest and most beautiful sunsets in the Indian Ocean. Another destination for a trip to the island's colonial past is The Sun House, with its pillar-lined covered veranda, which reigns high upon a hill. Up here, a Scottish spice trader, for whom the house was built in the mid-nineteenth century, found the best spot to watch for ships from his homeland. Today you can enjoy the knee-tremblingly beautiful view of the harbour but without the business worries. The six rooms in The Sun House are also simply beautiful; decorated entirely in white with a few dark accents. They have a wonderful way of making you feel like you are in your own living room – not in a hotel where there were guests before you and will be guests after you. In the gardens full of frangipanis and mango trees or at the pool, the days in the tropics drift past in a dream. But a word of warning: In the evening, the menus do full justice to the name "Spice Island of Sri Lanka" and the bottle of water always stands within easy reach.

Book to pack: "Cinnamon Gardens" by Shyam Selvadurai

The Sun House
18 Upper Dickson Road
Galle, Sri Lanka
Tel. +94 (91) 438 02 75
Fax +94 (91) 22226 24
Email: info@thesunhouse.com
Website: www.thesunhouse.com
www.great-escapes-hotels.com

DIRECTIONS	Situated 100 km/62 miles south of Colombo (travel time: 1.5 hr.) on the south coast of the island.
RATES	$$
ROOMS	4 small double rooms, 1 large double room, 1 Cinnamon Suite.
FOOD	"Cuisine of the Sun" – with influences from India, Malaysia, Portugal and Holland.
HISTORY	Built in the nineteenth century as a Scottish spice trader's residence, today it is a small boutique hotel.
X-FACTOR	Vacation of the best quality in colonial ambience.

Das weiße Haus

In Galle scheinen die Uhren in der Kolonialzeit stehengeblieben zu sein. Das langsam schlagende Herz des Städtchens an der Südküste von Sri Lanka ist das holländische Fort, wo hinter dicken Stadtmauern alte Kaufmannshäuser stehen, Oldtimer durch enge Straße knattern und man abends zur Star Bastion spaziert, um einen der kitschigschönsten Sonnenuntergänge im Indischen Ozean zu erleben. Ziel einer Reise in die koloniale Vergangenheit der Insel ist auch das Sun House, das mit seinen säulengesäumten und überdachten Veranden auf einem Hügel thront. Hier oben hatte der schottische Gewürzhändler, der das Haus Mitte des 19. Jahrhunderts bauen ließ, den besten Platz gefunden, um nach Schiffen aus seiner Heimat Ausschau zu halten – heute genießt man den zum Niederknien schönen Blick auf den Hafen aber eher ohne geschäftliche Verpflichtungen. Schlicht schön sind auch die sechs Zimmer des Sun House; ganz in Weiß gehalten und mit sparsamen dunklen Akzenten. Sie lassen einen auf wundersame Weise glauben, im eigenen Wohnzimmer zu sein – nicht in einem Hotel, in dem schon vorher Gäste da waren und auch nachher welche kommen werden. In den Gärten voller Frangipanis und Mangobäume oder am Pool plätschern die Tropentage traumhaft dahin. Aber Vorsicht: Abends machen die Menüs der Gewürzinsel Sri Lanka alle Ehre – die Flasche Wasser steht stets in Reichweite.

Buchtipp: »Die Zimtgärten« von Shyam Selvadurai

La maison blanche

A Galle, les pendules semblent s'être arrêtées à l'époque coloniale. Le cœur tranquille de la petite ville méridionale du Sri Lanka est le fort hollandais qui dissimule derrière ses murs d'enceinte d'anciennes maisons de négociants. Ici, on peut encore voir de vieilles automobiles pétarader dans les étroites ruelles et le soir on va se promener au Star Bastion afin d'admirer l'un des plus beaux couchers de soleil sur l'océan Indien. Ce voyage dans le passé colonial de l'île conduit aussi à la Sun House qui trône sur une colline, avec sa véranda entourée de colonnes. La maison a été construite au 19e siècle par un marchand d'épices écossais qui avait ainsi trouvé l'endroit idéal pour voir arriver ses bateaux venant d'Ecosse. Aujourd'hui, on jouit de la vue splendide sur le port sans arrière-pensée commerciale. Les six chambres de la Sun House sont aussi belles et sobres avec leur décoration blanche ponctuée seulement ici et là de touches sombres. Elles donnent au visiteur l'étonnante impression de se croire dans sa salle à manger et non pas dans une chambre d'hôtel où les clients se succèdent. Dans les jardins regorgeant de frangipaniers et de manguiers ou près de la piscine les journées sous les tropiques s'écoulent comme en rêve ; mais attention, le soir les menus de « l'île aux épices » font honneur à son nom. Mieux vaut avoir une bouteille d'eau à portée de main.

Livre à emporter : « Jardins de cannelle » de Shyam Selvadurai

ANREISE	100 km südlich von Colombo gelegen (Fahrtzeit: 1,5 h), an der Südküste der Insel.
PREIS	$$
ZIMMER	4 kleine Doppelzimmer, 1 großes Doppelzimmer, 1 Cinnamon-Suite.
KÜCHE	»Cuisine of the Sun« – gut gewürzt und mit Einflüssen aus Indien, Malaysia, Portugal und Holland.
GESCHICHTE	Im 19. Jahrhundert als Residenz eines schottischen Gewürzhändlers erbaut, heute ein kleines Boutique-Hotel.
X-FAKTOR	Ferien vom Feinsten im Kolonialambiente.

ACCÈS	Situé à 100 km au sud de Colombo (1 heure et demie de trajet), sur la côte méridionale de l'île.
PRIX	$$
CHAMBRES	4 petites chambres doubles, 1 grande chambre double, 1 suite Cinnamon.
RESTAURATION	«Cuisine of the Sun» – avec des influences de l'Inde, de la Malaisie, du Portugal et de Hollande.
HISTOIRE	Construite au 19e siècle pour un marchand d'épices écossais, la maison est aujourd'hui un petit hôtel.
LE « PETIT PLUS »	Un séjour de qualité dans une atmosphère coloniale.

A Storybook Island...
Taprobane Island, Galle

A Storybook Island

It is one of those photos that makes you close your eyes and pray that when you open them again you will be at the place in the picture. Warm salty air, waves rolling gently over the sand, an island packed with palm trees and on which there is only one house. Taprobane is a dream island *par excellence*, a dream that you might think could never come true. But unfulfilled dreams did not feature in the life of Count de Mauny. In 1922 this eccentric Brit and descendent of a general in Napoleon's army had a villa built on the island at Weligama Bay. It was intended to be not so much an enclosed house as a pavilion that was open to its surroundings as much as possible. And it really worked: spacious and sparingly furnished rooms are arranged around a hexagonal hall with projecting terraces that allow a 360-degree view. In the ensuing decades, a very artistic clientele enjoyed these premises. None other than Arthur C. Clarke said that this is where he was freed from the "tyranny of the keyboard" and learned to wear a sarong. Paul Bowles even went so far as to buy the island and wrote "The Spider's House" here and Peggy Guggenheim lay in the sun for days just at this spot. Today, the villa provides space for a maximum of 10 visitors and a new pool to experience their very own private Sri Lanka, which is appropriate since "Taprobane" was the Greek name for ancient Ceylon.

Book to pack: "The Spider's House" by Paul Bowles

Taprobane Island
Weligama
Sri Lanka
Tel. +94 (91) 438 02 75
Fax +94 (91) 222 26 24
Email: info@thesunhouse.com
www.taprobaneisland.com
www.great-escapes-hotels.com

DIRECTIONS	Situated on Sri Lanka's southern coast by Weligama (3 hours or a 1-hour flight from Colombo, transfer available upon request), passage by foot, elephant or palanquin.
RATES	$$$$
ROOMS	4 en-suite rooms, 1 suite (each with its own bath). Looked after by a service team (6 people).
FOOD	Curries from Sri Lanka; seafood and continental dishes.
HISTORY	Built in 1922 by Count de Mauny; a destination for many artists right up to the 1990s.
X-FACTOR	Own your own island just for once – even if only for a vacation.

Eine Bilderbuchinsel

Es ist eines jener Fotos, bei deren Anblick man die Augen schließt und betet, genau am Ort dieser Aufnahme zu stehen, wenn man sie wieder öffnet. Warme Salzluft, Wellen, die leise über den Sand rauschen, eine Insel, die von Palmen überquillt und auf der nur ein einziges Haus steht. Taprobane Island ist ein Sehnsuchtsziel par excellence, ein Traum, von dem man eigentlich annimmt, er könne nie Wirklichkeit werden. Doch unerfüllte Träume kamen im Leben des Count de Mauny nicht vor. 1922 ließ der exzentrische Brite und Nachfahre eines Generals in Napoleons Heer auf der Insel in der Weligama Bay eine Villa bauen, die weniger ein abgeschlossenes Haus werden sollte als vielmehr ein Pavillon, der sich der Umgebung so weit wie möglich öffnet. Rund um eine sechseckige Halle liegen Räume, die diesen Namen wirklich verdienen – großzügig und sparsam möbliert –, sowie ausladende Terrassen mit einem 360-Grad-Panorama. Das genoss in den folgenden Jahrzehnten eine künstlerische Klientel – Arthur C. Clarke wurde hier nach eigenen Aussagen von der »Tyrannei der Tastatur« befreit und lernte, einen Sarong zu tragen; Paul Bowles kaufte die Insel sogar und schrieb auf ihr »Das Haus der Spinne«; Peggy Guggenheim lag hier tagelang in der Sonne. Heute bietet die Villa maximal zehn Personen Platz, die im Haus und am neuen Pool ihr ganz privates Sri Lanka erleben – und das im wahrsten Sinne des Wortes: »Taprobane« ist der griechische Name für das alte Ceylon.

Buchtipp: »Das Haus der Spinne« von Paul Bowles

Une île enchantée

C'est le genre de photo que l'on regarde avant de fermer les yeux et de prier le ciel de se trouver exactement là en les rouvrant. Air chaud et salé, des vagues qui bruissent doucement sur le sable, une île plantée de palmiers à profusion et sur laquelle ne se dresse qu'une seule maison. S'il est un lieu auquel l'âme aspire, un rêve dont on croit qu'il ne deviendra jamais réalité, c'est bien Taprobane Island.

Il ne serait jamais venu à l'idée du comte de Mauny, descendant d'un général de l'armée napoléonienne, que ses désirs ne pussent être exaucés. En 1922, l'excentrique Anglais fit édifier sur l'île une villa dans la baie de Weligama. Il recherchait moins une maison fermée sur elle-même qu'un pavillon s'ouvrant le plus possible à la nature environnante. Tout autour d'une salle hexagonale se déploient des pièces aux proportions généreuses et sobrement meublées et de vastes terrasses qui offrent une vue circulaire sur l'île et la mer. Au fil du temps, de nombreux artistes ont su profiter de ce panorama fascinant – l'auteur de science-fiction Arthur C. Clarke a été libéré ici, selon ses dires, de « la tyrannie du clavier » et a appris à porter un sarong ; Paul Bowles, quant à lui, a même acheté l'île et a rédigé dans ces lieux « La maison de l'araignée » ; Peggy Guggenheim passait ici des journées entières au soleil.

Aujourd'hui, la villa offre le gîte et le couvert à dix personnes qui veulent découvrir Sri Lanka en toute liberté dans la maison et au bord de la nouvelle piscine et prendre le temps de vivre dans cette île qui a su préserver le nom sonore que les Grecs avaient donné à Ceylan : Taprobane.

Livre à emporter : « La maison de l'araignée » de Paul Bowles

ANREISE	An der Südküste Sri Lankas vor Weligama gelegen (3 Fahrt- oder 1 Flugstunde von Colombo entfernt, Transfer auf Wunsch), Passage zu Fuß, per Elefant oder Sänfte.
PREIS	$$$$
ZIMMER	4 Ensuite-Zimmer, 1 Suite (jeweils mit eigenem Bad). Betreut von einem Serviceteam (6 Personen).
KÜCHE	Currys aus Sri Lanka, Meeresfrüchte und kontinentale Gerichte.
GESCHICHTE	1922 vom Count de Mauny gebaut, bis in die neunziger Jahre Ziel vieler Künstler.
X-FAKTOR	Einmal Inselbesitzer sein – und sei es nur für einen Urlaub.

ACCÈS	Sur la côte sud du Sri Lanka, devant Weligama (à 3 h de voiture ou 1 h d'avion de Colombo), passage à pied, à dos d'éléphant ou en chaise à porteurs.
PRIX	$$$$
CHAMBRES	4 en-suite chambres et 1 suite (avec salle de bains annexe). Une équipe de 6 personnes veille au bien-être des hôtes.
RESTAURATION	Curries sri lankais, fruits de mer et plats continentaux.
HISTOIRE	Edifié en 1922 par le comte de Mauny. But de voyage de nombreux artistes jusqu'aux années 90.
LE « PETIT PLUS »	Posséder une île, rien qu'une fois, et ne serait-ce que pour y passer ses vacances.

Nature Pure...
Ulpotha, Galgiriyawa Mountains

Nature Pure

Ulpotha has never been short of legends: This small village
in the deepest Sri Lankan jungle is supposedly the holy
place, described in ancient myths, where Shiva's son had
a shrine built to which Prince Saliya and Asokamala fled
to live out their love which was not tolerated by the royal
palace. Even today, secrets and spirituality still play an
important role in Ulpotha – as a source of inspiration for
one of the most unusual eco-tourist projects in Asia. Two
private, non-profit organizations have rebuilt Ulpotha as a
traditional farming village with organic farm and reforesta-
tion project. With the help of old irrigation systems, traditional working methods and a large helping of idealism, the
aim is to bring back the original Ceylon. Ulpotha is only
open to visitors from November to March and in June/July –
where a mixture of eco-lodge, vacation camp and introduc-
tory courses in spiritual exercises await them. Yoga courses,
massages and Ayurveda are regular rituals filling the days,
which pass quietly and gently between the jungle, sea and
campfire site. Every visitor to Ulpotha will enjoy nature in
its purest form – and experience that as a luxury.
Book to pack: "Running in the Family" by Michael Ondaatje

Ulpotha
Flat 36
Galle Face Court 2
Colombo 03
Sri Lanka
Tel. +44 (208) 123 3603
Email: info@ulpotha.com
www.ulpotha.com
www.great-escapes-hotels.com

DIRECTIONS	Situated at the foot of the Galgiriyawa Mountains, 30 km/18 miles north of Kurunegala, 140 km/87 miles from Colombo Airport.
RATES	$$
ROOMS	A maximum of 19 guests live in 7 simple cottages (double rooms).
FOOD	Strictly vegetarian, with products from its own organic farm. Cooking is done over an open fire.
HISTORY	The legendary Ulpotha turns ambitious eco-tourist project.
X-FACTOR	Insights into Sri Lanka's soul.

Natur pur

An Legenden hat es Ulpotha noch nie gemangelt: Das kleine Dorf im tiefsten Dschungel von Sri Lanka soll der heilige
Ort sein, der in jahrtausendealten Mythen beschrieben ist.
Wo Shivas Sohn einen Schrein errichten ließ und wohin
Prinz Saliya und Asokamala flohen, um ihre vom Königs-
palast nicht geduldete Liebe zu leben. Auch heute noch
spielen Geheimnisse und Spiritualität eine wichtige Rolle
in Ulpotha – als Inspirationsquelle für eines der außer-
gewöhnlichsten Ökotourismus-Projekte Asiens. Zwei private und gemeinnützige Organisationen haben Ulpotha als
traditionelles Bauerndorf wieder aufgebaut, als Biofarm und
Aufforstungsbetrieb. Mit Hilfe alter Bewässerungssysteme,
überlieferten Arbeitsmethoden und einer großen Portion
Idealismus soll hier das ursprüngliche Ceylon wieder aufleben. Nur von November bis März sowie im Juni und Juli
ist Ulpotha für Besucher geöffnet – sie erwartet dann eine
Mischung aus Eco-Lodge, Feriencamp und Einführungskurs
in spirituelle Übungen. Yogakurse, Massagen und Ayurveda
sind feste Bestandteile der Tage, die zwischen Urwald, See
und Feuerstelle ruhig und sanft dahinfließen. Wer nach
Ulpotha kommt, soll die Natur in ihrer reinsten Form
erleben – und das als Luxus empfinden.

Buchtipp: »Es liegt in der Familie« von Michael Ondaatje

Pour les amoureux de la nature

Ulpotha est un lieu saint entouré de légendes. Selon les
mythes ancestraux, c'est là en effet, dans ce petit village
enfoui dans la jungle du Sri Lanka, que le fils de Shiva aurait
fait bâtir un mausolée et que le prince Saliya se serait réfugié
avec la belle Asokamala pour fuir les foudres de son père qui
désapprouvait cet amour. Mais les mystères et la spiritualité
jouent aujourd'hui encore un rôle important à Ulpotha – et
ils ont inspiré l'un des projets de tourisme écologique les
plus exceptionnels d'Asie. Deux organisations privées d'uti-
lité publique ont reconstruit Ulpotha en village traditionnel,
lui ajoutant une ferme bio et une entreprise de reboisement.
Le but est de faire revivre le Ceylan d'origine tout en s'aidant
de systèmes d'irrigation, de méthodes de travail classiques et
d'une bonne dose d'idéalisme. Ouvert aux visiteurs de
novembre à mars et durant les mois de juin et de juillet,
Ulpotha est un mélange de lodge écologique, de camp de
vacances et de cours d'initiation aux exercices spirituels. Le
yoga, les massages et l'Ayurvéda rythment les journées qui
s'écoulent paisiblement avec pour toile de fond la végétation
luxuriante, les eaux du lac et les feux de camp. Celui qui
vient à Ulpotha découvrira la nature sous sa forme originelle
et la percevra comme un luxe.

Livre à emporter : « Un air de famille » de Michael Ondaatje

ANREISE	Am Fuß der Galgiriyawa Mountains gelegen, 30 km nörd-lich von Kurunegala, 140 km vom Flughafen Colombo entfernt.
PREIS	$$
ZIMMER	Maximal 19 Gäste wohnen in 7 einfachen Cottages (Dop-pelzimmer).
KÜCHE	Ausschließlich vegetarisch und mit Produkten aus eige-nem Bio-Anbau. Gekocht wird über dem offenen Feuer.
GESCHICHTE	Aus dem sagenhaften Ort Ulpotha wurde in den neun-ziger Jahren ein ambitioniertes Ökotourismus-Projekt.
X-FAKTOR	Einblicke in Sri Lankas Seele.

ACCÈS	Au pied du Galgiriyawa, à 30 km au nord de Kurunega-la et à 140 km de l'aéroport de Colombo.
PRIX	$$
CHAMBRES	19 hôtes au maximum résident dans 7 cottages simples (chambre double).
RESTAURATION	Exclusivement végétarienne avec des produits bios cultivés sur place. Cuisine au feu de bois.
HISTOIRE	Le lieu légendaire d'Ulpotha est devenu dans les années 90 un projet de tourisme écologique ambitieux.
LE « PETIT PLUS »	Incursion dans l'âme du Sri Lanka.

The Jewel by the Silver Lake...

Inle Princess Resort, Inle Lake

The Jewel by the Silver Lake

They emit the fine scent of resin and forest, soft light and even on cool days, a certain warmth: Wooden houses are something very special, something in which one feels at home even in a distant land. A perfect example of this phenomenon is the Inle Princess Resort on the shores of Inle Lake. It features 42 chalets, whose colour reminds one of dark, runny honey. Some of the chalets stand on stilts over the glassy water while others have a view of the dark greenery on the shores. Under the low roofs, you can live relatively simply, but with all of the necessary comforts. Regardless of where you sit to eat at one of the restaurant tables on the landing stage, you always have a view of a rural idyll that looks as if it had been drawn on delicate silk. Inle Lake is paradise rediscovered, a sort of gap in time far from everything that takes place the world. It is Myanmar at its most unspoilt. For countless generations, friendly old women have woven silk here, boats bearing fruit-and-vegetable markets or palatial decks have floated past and the men have mastered a unique one-legged rowing technique – visitors fall in the water at the mere thought of this type of movement. Guests at the Inle Princess Resort can also pleasantly fill their days with walks in the Shan hills, go bird watching or admire the sunset from their covered veranda, which is so beautiful that one hardly dares breathe. But do it anyway, because every second spent without this wonderful fragrance of water, rattan and wood is one too many.

Book to pack: "The Piano Tuner" by Daniel Mason

Inle Princess Resort
Magyizin Village
Inle Lake
Myanmar
Tel. +95 (81) 290 55
Fax +95 (81) 293 63
Email: ipresort@yangon.net.mm
Website: www.inleprincessresort.com
www.great-escapes-hotels.com

DIRECTIONS	Situated on the east shore of Lake Inle, 30 km / 19 miles from Heho Airport (daily connections from Mandalay and Yangon, 20 to 60 min.).
RATES	$$
ROOMS	42 chalets.
FOOD	Menus from Myanmar.
HISTORY	Based on the typical houses built on stilts in the region.
X-FACTOR	Where you come closest to nature.

Der Schatz am Silbersee

Sie verströmen einen feinen Duft nach Harz und Wald, weiches Licht und selbst an kühlen Tagen eine gewisse Wärme: Holzhäuser sind etwas ganz Besonderes; etwas, wo man sich sogar in einem fernen Land wie zuhause fühlt. Ein Musterbeispiel für dieses Phänomen ist das Inle Princess Resort am Ufer des Inle Sees – mit 42 Chalets, deren Farbe an flüssigen dunklen Honig erinnert und von denen einige auf Stelzen über dem spiegelglatten Wasser stehen, während andere auf dichtes Ufergrün blicken. Unter den tief gezogenen Dächern wohnt man vergleichsweise schlicht, aber doch mit allem nötigen Komfort, setzt sich zum Essen an einen der Restauranttische auf dem Steg und sieht von wo aus auch immer ein ländliches Idyll wie auf zarte Seide gemalt. Der Inle See ist ein wieder entdecktes Paradies, eine Art Zeitloch fern jeglichen Weltgeschehens und das ursprünglichste Myanmar. Seit ungezählten Generationen weben hier freundliche alte Frauen Seide, schwimmen Obst- und Gemüsemärkte oder Boote mit palastartigen Aufsätzen vorbei und beherrschen die Männer eine einzigartige einbeinige Rudertechnik – Besucher fallen beim bloßen Gedanken an diese Kunst der Fortbewegung ins Wasser. Gäste des Inle Princess Resorts können ihre Tage auch mit Wanderungen in den Shan-Hügeln angenehm füllen, auf Vogelbeobachtung gehen oder von ihrer überdachten Veranda aus den Sonnenuntergang bewundern, der so schön ist, dass man kaum zu atmen wagt. Tun Sie es trotzdem, denn jede Sekunde ohne diesen wunderbaren Geruch nach Wasser, Rattan und Holz ist eine zu viel.

**Buchtipp: »Der Klavierstimmer Ihrer Majestät«
von Daniel Mason**

Ô temps! Suspends ton vol...

Les maisons de bois embaument la résine et la forêt, elles laissent pénétrer une douce lumière et la température y reste agréable lorsque les journées sont fraîches. On s'y sent chez soi, même à l'autre bout du monde. Le Inle Princess Resort sur les rives du lac Inlé confirme ce phénomène avec ses 42 habitations dont la couleur évoque le miel liquide et sombre. Certaines se dressent sur des pilotis au-dessus du miroir de l'eau et d'autres ont une vue sur la rive où se déploie une végétation luxuriante. Sous les toits bas, les maisons sont aménagées de manière relativement modeste mais elles sont dotées du confort nécessaire. On prend ses repas au restaurant situé sur la passerelle, entouré d'un paysage idyllique qui semble dessiné au pinceau sur de la soie. Le lac Inlé est un paradis retrouvé, un « trou dans le temps », loin du monde moderne. C'est aussi le Myanmar dans ce qu'il a de plus authentique. Ici, depuis d'innombrables générations, les vieilles femmes aimables tissent de la soie, des marchés flottants de fruits et de légumes ou des embarcations aux airs de palais circulent sur les eaux, les hommes maîtrisent une technique unique en ramant sur une jambe – les visiteurs en restent abasourdis.

Les clients du Inle Princess Resort peuvent aussi passer d'agréables journées en partant en randonnée dans les collines Shan ou observer les oiseaux. Ils peuvent aussi admirer de leur véranda le coucher de soleil, si beau qu'on ose à peine respirer. Faites-le quand même – chaque seconde passée sans sentir cette odeur sublime d'eau, de rotin et de bois est une seconde perdue pour vous.

Livre à emporter : « L'Accordeur de piano » de Daniel Mason

ANREISE	Am Ostufer des Inle Sees gelegen, 30 km vom Flughafen Heho entfernt (tägliche Verbindungen ab Mandalay und Yangon, 20 bis 60 min).
PREIS	$$
ZIMMER	42 Chalets.
KÜCHE	Menüs aus Myanmar.
GESCHICHTE	Den typischen Pfahlbauten der Region nachempfunden.
X-FAKTOR	Wo man der Natur am nächsten kommt.

ACCÈS	Situé sur la rive orientale du lac Inlé, à 30 km de l'aéroport de Hého (liaisons quotidiennes à partir de Mandalay et de Yangon, 20 à 60 min).
PRIX	$$
CHAMBRES	42 maisons de bois.
RESTAURATION	Cuisine traditionnelle du Myanmar.
HISTOIRE	Habitations inspirées des maisons sur pilotis caractéristiques de la région.
LE « PETIT PLUS »	La nature n'est jamais bien loin.

The Flow of Change...
Road to Mandalay, Yangon

The Flow of Change

One might think that the only thing the Rhine, Elbe and Ayeyarvadi have in common is that they are rivers. But the three waterways are also linked by a ship, which in the 1960s rolled past the Loreley as a steamboat, was later anchored in Dresden as a floating hotel and then was sold to distant Asia: Today the "Road to Mandalay" is Myanmar's most famous river cruise ship. The shipping company invested six million dollars in turning the boat made in Germany into an Asian dream with local handcrafted art and antiques, handmade furniture and an observation platform for afternoon tea. If you board the ship, you drift through the fairytale world of Myanmar, far from the aftermath of General Ne Win's socialist course, the struggles of Aung San Suu Kyi and the uncertain path that the whole nation is taking into the future – the "Road to Mandalay" travels through another world. Here tourism emerges as if in slow motion, showing shining gold pagodas, ancient temples and riverside settlements in a way that is both proud and timid. During the luxurious days on deck one feels like an adventurer and on some nights there are magical surprises: Thousands of Chinese lanterns float on the Ayeyarvadi and fetch the stars from the sky onto the water.

Book to pack: "The Glass Palace" by Amitav Ghosh

Road to Mandalay
Office USA
10 Weybosset Street, Suite 500
Providence, Rhode Island 02903
Tel. +1 (401) 351 75 18
Website: www.orient-express.com
www.great-escapes-hotels.com

DIRECTIONS	Individual journey to Mandalay or Bagan. The "Road to Mandalay" sails between July and April.
RATES	$$$$
Cabins	14 Single Cabins, 38 Superior Cabins, 14 State Cabins.
FOOD	Asian and European.
HISTORY	Since 1996 a luxury cruiser.
X-FACTOR	Time travel in slow motion through unknown country.

Fließender Wechsel

Die Gemeinsamkeit von Rhein, Elbe und Ayeyarwady erschöpft sich darin, dass alle drei Flüsse sind – könnte man meinen. Doch die drei Wasserwege verbindet auch ein Schiff, das in den sechziger Jahren als Rheindampfer an der Loreley vorbeischaukelte, später als schwimmendes Hotel in Dresden vor Anker lag und dann ins ferne Asien verkauft wurde: Die »Road to Mandalay« ist heute das berühmteste Flusskreuzfahrtschiff Myanmars. Sechs Millionen Dollar investierte die Reederei, um das Boot made in Germany in einen asiatischen Traum zu verwandeln, mit einheimischem Kunsthandwerk und Antiquitäten, handgefertigen Möbeln und einer Aussichtsplattform für den Afternoon-Tea. Wer an Bord geht, gleitet durch das Märchenland Myanmar; weit entfernt von den Nachwehen, die der sozialistische Kurs des Generals Ne Win hinterlassen hat, den Kämpfen der Aung San Suu Kyi und dem unsicheren Weg einer ganzen Nation in ihre Zukunft – die »Road to Mandalay« fährt durch eine andere Welt. Dort öffnet man sich wie in Zeitlupe dem Tourismus, zeigt goldglänzende Pagoden, alte Tempel und Ufersiedlungen stolz und scheu zugleich her. Ein Hauch von Entdeckerleben liegt über den luxuriösen Tagen an Deck, und in manchen Nächten warten zauberhafte Überraschungen: Dann treiben tausende von Lampions auf dem Ayeyarvadi und holen die Sterne vom Himmel aufs Wasser.

Buchtipp: »Der Glaspalast« von Amitav Ghosh

« Come you back to Mandalay »

Que peuvent bien avoir l'Elbe, le Rhin et l'Irrawaddy en commun ? Et bien ces trois fleuves ont vu le même navire circuler sur leurs eaux. Celui-ci a côtoyé la Loreley au cours des années soixante, alors qu'il était navire de croisière sur le Rhin. Plus tard, il est devenu un hôtel flottant à Dresde avant d'être acheté par une compagnie asiatique. Aujourd'hui, le « Road to Mandalay » – un clin d'œil au poème de Kipling –, est le plus célèbre navire de croisière du Myanmar, l'ancienne Birmanie.

L'armateur a investi six millions de dollars pour transformer l'embarcation « made in Germany » en rêve exotique abritant des objets réalisés par les artisans du pays et des antiquités, des meubles fabriqués à la main et offrant une plateforme avec vue panoramique où l'on peut prendre le thé de cinq heures. Celui qui monte à bord glisse à travers un pays de contes de fées, bien loin des séquelles de la junte militaire du général Ne Win, des combats de Aung San Suu Kyi et de l'avenir incertain de toute une nation. Le « Road to Mandalay » navigue dans un autre univers.

Ce pays s'ouvre lentement, très lentement, au tourisme, à qui il présente avec une timidité teintée de fierté ses stûpas dorés, ses temples anciens et des petits villages perchés sur les rives. Ceux qui vivent si luxueusement sur le pont se sentent une âme d'explorateur et quelquefois, la nuit, des surprises enchanteresses les attendent, par exemple lorsque des milliers de lampions flottent sur l'Irrawaddy, comme si les étoiles y étaient tombées.

Livre à emporter : « Le palais des miroirs » d'Amitav Ghosh

ANREISE	Individuelle Anreise nach Mandalay oder Bagan. Die »Road to Mandalay« fährt von Juli bis April.
PREIS	$$$$
KABINEN	14 Einzelkabinen, 38 Superior-Kabinen, 14 State-Kabinen.
KÜCHE	Asiatisch und europäisch.
GESCHICHTE	Seit 1996 ein Luxuskreuzer.
X-FAKTOR	Zeitreise in Zeitlupe durch ein unbekanntes Land.

ACCÈS	Voyage individuel à destination de Mandalay ou Bagan. Le « Road to Mandalay » circule du mois de juillet au mois d'avril.
PRIX	$$$$
CABINES	14 cabines individuelles, 38 cabines doubles (Superior), 14 cabines de luxe (State).
RESTAURATION	Cuisine asiatique et européenne.
HISTOIRE	Navire de croisière luxueux depuis 1996.
LE « PETIT PLUS »	Un voyage au ralenti en pays inconnu.

Enchanted Gardens...
Bagan Hotel, Bagan

Enchanted Gardens

The first king of Bagan's greatest fears were not war, sickness or even the disfavour of his people: Thammoddarit was afraid of tigers, flying squirrels, boars, birds and gourd plants. It was the last one that mainly kept him awake nights, because night after night they grew like in a time-lapse photograph, slowly covering the country, enabling the feared animals to live a life of paradise – until a brave man named Pyusawhti drew his bow and fatally wounded all five "dangers." As a reward, he was allowed to marry Thammoddarit's daughter and years later become king himself. On that very day, he had pagodas built on all five spots where he had once conquered the animal and plant world – a good foundation! Today Bagan is one of the greatest archaeological sites in Asia. Over an area of about 35 square kilometres, one can visit 5000 temple ruins and almost 70 restored holy relics. One of the best places to start is the Bagan Hotel, which is situated at the foot of the Gawdawpalin Temple and directly on the shores of the Ayeyarwady, just a few steps away from Old Bagan's archaeological museum. The buildings of red-brown stone are linked by small paths and situated in the midst of enchanted gardens. If you take a little time for exploration, you will be surprised by a statue of Buddha behind just about every corner and in almost every room, and after a few days you will feel like picking up a shovel and brush and taking part in the excavations in and around Bagan. But pulling up supposed weeds is hardly worth it – a king no longer reigns over the city with a daughter of marriageable age.

Book to pack: "Freedom From Fear and Other Writings"
by Aung San Suu Kyi

Bagan Hotel
Bagan, Old Bagan, Myanmar
Tel. +95 61 600 32
Fax +95 15 011 23
Email: olbagho2@baganmail.net.mm
Website: www.bagan-hotel.com
www.great-escapes-hotels.com

DIRECTIONS	Situated in Old Bagan and directly on the banks of the Ayeyarwady, 16 km / 10 miles west of Nyaung U Airport.
RATES	$
ROOMS	50 Superior Rooms, 36 Deluxe Rooms, 12 Junior Suites, 4 Bagan Suites, 4 Riverview Suites.
FOOD	Good traditional specialties from Myanmar as well as Western dishes.
HISTORY	Built on historical ground and at the foot of the pagodas.
X-FACTOR	Living like in a giant open-air museum.

Die Spur der Steine

Die größte Angst des ersten Königs von Bagan war nicht Krieg, nicht Krankheit und auch nicht die Ungnade seines Volkes: Thammoddarit fürchtete sich vor Tigern, Flughörnchen, Ebern, Vögeln und Kürbispflanzen. Vor allem letztere raubten ihm den Schlaf, da sie Nacht für Nacht wie im Zeitraffer das Land überwucherten und den gefürchteten Tieren ein paradiesisches Leben ermöglichten – bis ein tapferer Mann namens Pyusawhti seinen magischen Bogen spannte und alle fünf »Gefahren« tödlich traf. Zum Dank durfte er die Tochter Thammoddarits heiraten und Jahre später selbst den Thron besteigen. An diesem Tag ließ er an allen fünf Stellen Pagoden errichten, an denen er einst über die Tier- und Pflanzenwelt gesiegt hatte – ein guter Grundstock! Heute ist Bagan eine der größten archäologischen Stätten Asiens – auf rund 35 Quadratkilometern kann man 5000 Ruinen und knapp 70 restaurierte Heiligtümer besichtigen. Einer der besten Ausgangspunkte ist das Bagan Hotel, das zu Füßen des Gawdawpalin Tempels und direkt am Ufer des Ayeyarwady steht, nur wenige Schritte vom Archäologischen Museum Old Bagans entfernt. Die Gebäude aus rotbraunem Stein liegen inmitten verwunschener Gärten und sind durch schmale Pfade miteinander verbunden – wer sich Zeit für Entdeckungen nimmt, wird hinter beinahe jeder Ecke und in fast jedem Zimmer von einer Statue des Buddha überrascht und bekommt nach ein paar Tagen Lust, bei den Ausgrabungen in und um Bagan selbst Schaufel und Pinsel in die Hand zu nehmen. Das Zupfen vermeintlichen Unkrauts lohnt sich allerdings kaum – über die Stadt herrscht kein König mit heiratsfähiger Tochter mehr.

Buchtipp: »Der Weg zur Freiheit« von Aung San Suu Kyi

Les jardins enchantés

Le premier roi du Bagan ne redoutait ni la guerre, ni la maladie pas plus qu'il n'avait peur de tomber en disgrâce auprès de son peuple. En revanche Thammoddarit craignait plus que tout au monde le tigre, les écureuils volants, les verrats, les oiseaux et les courges. Ces dernières en particulier l'empêchaient de dormir car, nuit après nuit, elles pullulaient à une telle rapidité que tout le pays en était envahi et qu'elles offraient un abri aux animaux indésirables. Un jour toutefois arriva un jeune homme courageux, qui s'appelait Pyusawhti. Bandant son arc magique, il transperça les cinq « dangers ». Pour le remercier, Thammoddarit lui accorda la main de sa fille et, plusieurs années plus tard, Pyusawhti monta sur le trône. Ce jour-là, il fit ériger des pagodes aux cinq endroits où il avait jadis vaincu le monde animal et végétal. Bagan est l'un des sites archéologiques les plus vastes d'Asie, il s'étend sur trente-cinq kilomètres carrés et compte cinq milles temples en ruines ainsi que soixante-dix sanctuaires restaurés. Celui qui désire visiter le site prendra comme point d'attache le Bagan Hotel, situé au pied du temple Gawdawpalin, sur les rives de l'Irrawaddy et à quelques pas seulement du musée archéologique Old Bagan. Les constructions en pierre brun-rouge sont nichées au milieu de jardins enchanteurs et reliées entre elles par d'étroits sentiers. Le visiteur désireux de partir à la découverte sera surpris de trouver une statue de Bouddha à chaque détour du chemin et dans presque toutes les chambres. Au bout de quelques jours, l'envie lui viendra de participer aux fouilles effectuées à Bagan et dans les alentours. Il se gardera toutefois d'arracher les plantes envahissantes car il n'y a plus de roi ayant une fille en âge de se marier.

Livre à emporter : « Nationalisme et littérature en Birmanie : Quelques aspects de la vie intellectuelle sous le colonialisme » d'Aung San Suu Kyi

ANREISE	In Old Bagan und direkt am Ufer des Ayeyarwady gelegen, 16 km westlich des Flughafens Nyaung U.
PREIS	$
ZIMMER	50 Superior Rooms, 36 Deluxe Rooms, 12 Junior-Suiten, 4 Bagan-Suiten, 4 Riverview-Suiten.
KÜCHE	Gute traditionelle Spezialitäten aus Myanmar, außerdem westliche Gerichte.
GESCHICHTE	Auf historischem Boden zu Füßen der Pagoden gebaut.
X-FAKTOR	Wohnen wie in einem riesigen Freiluftmuseum.

ACCÈS	Situé à Old Bagan, sur les rives de l'Irrawaddy, à 16 km à l'ouest de l'aéroport de Nyaung U.
PRIX	$
CHAMBRES	50 Superior Rooms, 36 Deluxe Rooms, 12 Junior Suites, 4 Bagan Suites, 4 Riverview Suites.
RESTAURATION	Spécialités traditionnelles de Myanmar, ainsi que plats occidentaux.
HISTOIRE	Construit sur un site historique au pied des pagodes.
LE « PETIT PLUS »	On se croirait dans un immense musée en plein air.

Under Buddha's Spell...
The Strand Hotel, Yangon

Under Buddha's Spell

Travelling to Myanmar generally promises a trip back in time, but the country also has places where the future is already part of the present. Particularly ahead is the capital Yangon: Only a few years ago, time passed slowly here and life on the streets only occasionally woke from its slumber. But today street traders, hectic flickering billboards and thousands of honking cars keep the city's pulse racing at all times. On some days, even the Shwedagon Pagoda has trouble maintaining its exalted aura. Local and foreign pilgrims stroll around and around this almost 100-meter-high shining gold symbol – whose foundations are said to contain eight hairs of Buddha – as if they wanted to transform the world wonder into a beehive. On the other hand, the Strand Hotel that is located directly by the river guarantees a peace and quiet that really does you good. It's no coincidence that its Victorian-style facade is reminiscent of Grand Hotels like Raffles or Fullerton in Singapore. The building was erected in 1901 as part of an Asian luxury hotel chain and has maintained its colonial charm ever since. Guests reside in spacious rooms with brilliantly polished teakwood parquet; you can happily listen to the quiet whirring of the ventilator for hours and admire the local art and antiques. During dinner, the crystal chandelier and splendid furniture almost make it hard to concentrate on your food; and the lobby is a dream of wood and marble. Here life passes by as if one were inside a pleasantly steamy bell jar – and the city beyond the doors were a distant memory.

Book to pack: "Burmese Days" by George Orwell

The Strand Hotel		
92 Strand Road	DIRECTIONS	Situated directly on the Yangon River and in the city's commercial and diplomat quarter, 10 km/6 miles south of the airport.
Yangon, Myanmar		
Tel. +95 (1) 24 33 77	RATES	$$$$
Fax +95 (1) 24 33 93	ROOMS	23 Deluxe Suites, 8 Superior Suites, 1 The Strand Suite.
Email: strand@ghmhotels.com	FOOD	The Strand Café and The Strand Grill are elegant and feature menus from Myanmar, afternoon tea and jazz. There is also a bar in the lounge in the lobby.
Website: www.ghmhotels.com	HISTORY	Opened in 1901 as a Grand Hotel.
www.great-escapes-hotels.com	X-FACTOR	The charm and luxury of the colonial period.

Im Bannkreis des Buddha

Myanmar verspricht normalerweise Reisen in die Vergangenheit – doch das Land besitzt auch Orte, an denen die Zukunft bereits Gegenwart ist. Allen voran die Hauptstadt Yangon: Wo noch vor einigen Jahren die Uhren langsam gingen und das Leben auf den Straßen nur gelegentlich aus seinem Halbschlaf erwachte, sorgen heute fliegende Händler, hektisch flimmernde Reklametafeln und tausende hupende Autos für einen dauerhaft hohen Puls. Selbst die Shwedagon-Pagode hat an manchen Tagen Mühe, ihre erhabene Aura zu bewahren – rund um das fast 100 Meter hohe, goldglänzende Wahrzeichen, in dessen Fundament acht Haare Buddhas eingebettet sein sollen, wandeln einheimische und fremde Pilger, als wollten sie das Weltwunder in einen Bienenstock verwandeln. Wirklich wohltuende Ruhe verspricht dagegen The Strand Hotel, das direkt am Fluss steht. Seine viktorianisch angehauchte Fassade erinnert nicht zufällig an Grand Hotels wie das Raffles oder das Fullerton in Singapur – das Gebäude wurde 1901 als Part einer asiatischen Luxushotelkette gebaut und hat sich seinen kolonialen Charme bis heute bewahrt. Man wohnt in weitläufigen Zimmern mit auf Hochglanz poliertem Teakholzparkett, könnte dem leise surrenden Ventilator stundenlang zuhören und bewundert einheimische Kunst sowie Antiquitäten. Beim Dinner fällt es fast schwer, sich angesichts der Kristalllüster und prachtvollen Möbel aufs Essen zu konzentrieren, und die Lobby ist ein Traum aus Holz und Marmor. Hier verläuft das Leben wie unter einer angenehm dämpfenden Glasglocke – die Stadt draußen vor den Toren verschwindet in der Ferne.

Buchtipp: »Tage in Burma« von George Orwell

Au pays du Dragon d'or

Normalement, le Myanmar promet un voyage dans le temps, mais le pays abrite aussi des lieux où l'avenir est déjà bien présent. C'est surtout le cas à Yangon, la capitale : là où les pendules n'avançaient que lentement il y a quelques années et où la rue ne s'éveillait qu'à l'occasion de son demi-sommeil, des marchands ambulants, des réclames scintillantes et des milliers de voitures qui klaxonnent, veillent aujourd'hui à ce que la ville vive à cent à l'heure. Même la paya Shwedagon, le sanctuaire le plus sacré où se trouveraient huit cheveux de Bouddha, a de la peine certains jours à garder sa sérénité. Autour du stupa d'une centaine de mètres de haut qui brille de tout l'éclat de l'or, les pèlerins et les visiteurs de toutes les nations affluent, transformant cette merveille en ruche bourdonnante.

The Strand Hotel, situé sur la rive du fleuve, promet en revanche un calme vraiment bienfaisant. Ce n'est pas un hasard si sa façade aux accents victoriens évoque de grands hôtels comme le Raffles ou le Fullerton de Singapour. En effet, le bâtiment qui faisait partie d'une chaîne d'hôtels de luxe asiatique a été édifié en 1901 et a su garder jusqu'à ce jour son charme colonial. On dort dans de vastes chambres aux parquets en teck polis, on pourrait écouter des heures durant le ronronnement du ventilateur et on admire l'art régional et les antiquités.

Il est bien difficile de se concentrer sur son dîner sous les lustres de cristal de la salle au manger magnifiquement meublée, quant au hall de l'hôtel, c'est un rêve de bois et de marbre. Habiter ici, c'est vivre comme sous une cloche qui amortit agréablement tous les bruits extérieurs – la ville, là-bas, n'est plus qu'un souvenir.

Livre à emporter : « Une histoire birmane » de George Orwell

ANREISE	Direkt am Yangon River und im Handels- und Diplomatenviertel der Stadt gelegen, 10 km südlich des Flughafens.
PREIS	$$$$
ZIMMER	23 Deluxe-Suiten, 8 Superior-Suiten, 1 The-Strand-Suite.
KÜCHE	Elegantes The Strand -Café und The -Strand-Grill mit Menüs aus Myanmar, Afternoon-Tea und Jazz. Außerdem eine Bar in der Lobby Lounge.
GESCHICHTE	1901 als Grand Hotel eröffnet.
X-FAKTOR	Der Charme und Luxus der Kolonialzeit.

ACCÈS	Situé sur la rive du Yangon, dans le quartier commercial et diplomatique de la ville, à 10 km au sud de l'aéroport.
PRIX	$$$$
CHAMBRES	23 Deluxe Suites, 8 Superior Suites, 1 The Strand Suite.
RESTAURATION	Elégant The Strand Café et The Strand Grill offrant des plats traditionnels du Myanmar, thé de cinq heures et jazz ainsi qu'un bar dans la Lobby Lounge.
HISTOIRE	Ouvert en 1901 en tant que Grand Hotel.
LE « PETIT PLUS »	L'époque coloniale et ses attraits.

Journey into the Past

Eastern & Oriental Express, Bangkok

Journey into the Past

There are not many ways to stop time and yet let it flow
(or rather: roll) past – the Eastern & Oriental Express is one
of them. Boarding one of the shiny green trains with the
cream-coloured window frames transports you directly from
the third millennium back to colonial times. You can sit on
velvet and silk or upholstered rattan, admire wooden inlays
with Far Eastern motifs or Thai lacquer work, sip Early Grey
tea in the afternoon or spread clotted cream onto scones –
the sort of ambience where a linen suit is *de rigeur*. The Eastern & Oriental Express has been travelling from Singapore
to Bangkok and from Bangkok to Chiang Mai since 1993, a
continuation of the era and success of the legendary Venice
Simplon-Orient-Express, which was the first train with
which passengers could travel directly from Singapore and
Kuala Lumpur to Bangkok. Like a slightly stumbling snake,
the 400-meter-long train rolls through the long river valleys,
past rice fields, jungles and ancient temples. *En route* there
is certainly no lack of vantage points: Every compartment
looks directly out onto the passing landscape; the windows
of the restaurant car have been especially enlarged, and on
the observation carriage there are not even panes of glass
to separate you from the great outdoors – it is entirely open.
**Book to pack: "Touch the Dragon: A Year in Thailand"
by Karen Connelly**

Eastern & Oriental Express

Office USA

10 Weybosset Street, Suite 500

Providence, Rhode Island 02903

Tel. +1 (401) 351 75 18

Website: www.orient-express.com

www.great-escapes-hotels.com

DIRECTIONS	Individual trip to Bangkok, Singapore or Chiang Mai.
RATES	$$$$
ROOMS	66 compartments, including 36 Pullman compartments, 28 state compartments and 2 presidential suites.
FOOD	Two restaurant cars with European-Asian cuisine.
HISTORY	In operation since September 1993.
X-FACTOR	Travelling like in the old days – but with all mod cons.

Reise in die Vergangenheit

Es gibt nicht viele Möglichkeiten, die Zeit anzuhalten und sie trotzdem fließen oder besser: rollen zu lassen – der Eastern & Oriental Express ist eine davon. Wer an Bord eines der grün glänzenden Waggons mit den cremefarben umrandeten Fenstern geht, reist vom dritten Jahrtausend direkt in die Kolonialzeit. Man sitzt auf Samt und Seide oder gepolstertem Rattan, bewundert Holzintarsien mit fernöstlichen Motiven oder thailändische Lackarbeiten, nippt nachmittags am Earl Grey oder bestreicht Scones mit clotted cream – keine Frage, dass in diesem Ambiente der Leinenanzug gleichsam Pflicht ist ... Der Eastern & Oriental Express fährt seit 1993 von Singapur nach Bangkok und von Bangkok nach Chiang Mai. Er knüpft damit an die Ära und die Erfolge des legendären Venice-Simplon-Orient-Express' an – des ersten Zuges, mit dem Passagiere direkt von Singapur und Kuala Lumpur nach Bangkok reisen konnten. Wie eine sich leicht ruckhaft fortbewegende Schlange rollt die 400 Meter lange Bahn durch ausgedehnte Flusstäler, vorbei an Reisfeldern, Urwäldern und alten Tempeln. An passenden Aussichtspunkten mangelt es unterwegs übrigens nicht: Jedes Abteil blickt direkt ins Freie, bei einem Umbau vergrößerte man die Fenster der Restaurantwagen, und auf dem Aussichtswagen trennen nicht einmal mehr Glasscheiben Drinnen und Draußen – er ist rundum offen.

Buchtipp: »Der Kuss des Drachen« von Karen Connelly

Luxe et nostalgie

Le Eastern & Oriental Express relève un défi incroyable qui est d'arrêter le temps tout en le laissant s'écouler. Le voyageur qui s'embarque à bord de ce train aux wagons verts étincelants et aux fenêtres encadrées de couleur crème a l'impression, en effet, de passer directement du troisième millénaire à l'époque coloniale. Assis sur des sièges en velours et en soie ou en osier capitonné, il peut admirer les marqueteries orientales ou les objet d'art en laque thaïlandais et déguster à petites gorgées son Earl Grey tout en recouvrant ses scones de clotted cream – il va sans dire que le costume chic, en lin bien entendu, est indispensable dans cet environnement. Le Eastern & Oriental Express effectue depuis 1993 le trajet de Singapour à Bangkok et de Bangkok à Chiang Mai, se rattachant ainsi à l'époque glorieuse du légendaire Venice Simplon-Orient-Express, le premier train qui reliait directement Singapour et Kuala Lumpur à Bangkok. Tel un serpent ondulant de 400 mètres, le train traverse de vastes vallées fluviales et longe les rizières, les forêts tropicales et les temples anciens. Les passagers peuvent d'ailleurs contempler le paysage en de multiples endroits : chaque cabine donne directement sur l'extérieur, les fenêtres du wagon-restaurant ont été élargies tout spécialement et dans le compartiment panoramique, aucune vitre ne fait obstacle à la vue : il est ouvert de tous les côtés.

Livre à emporter : « Du printemps la rosée. Voyages en Extrême-Orient » de Cees Nooteboom

ANREISE	Individuelle Anreise nach Bangkok, Singapur oder Chiang Mai.
PREIS	$$$$
ZIMMER	66 Abteile, darunter 36 Pullmann-Abteile, 28 State-Abteile und 2 Presidential-Suiten.
KÜCHE	Zwei Restaurantwagen mit europäisch-asiatischer Küche.
GESCHICHTE	Seit September 1993 auf Fahrt.
X-FAKTOR	Reisen wie anno dazumal – aber mit allem Komfort.

ACCÈS	Transport individuel à Bangkok, Singapour ou Chiang Mai.
PRIX	$$$$
CHAMBRES	66 compartiments, dont 36 cabines pullmann, 28 cabines state et 2 suites présidentielles.
RESTAURATION	Deux wagons-restaurants proposant une cuisine européenne et asiatique.
HISTOIRE	En service depuis septembre 1993.
LE « PETIT PLUS »	Voyager comme autrefois – le luxe en plus.

EASTERN & ORIENTAL EXPRESS

The Wellspring of Light...

Four Seasons Resort Chiang Mai, Chiang Mai

The Wellspring of Light

Every morning the gods let gold dust rain on Chiang Mai. When shortly before dawn the torches flare up, the papyrus lanterns gently swing back and forth and the lanterns emit a fragile glow; the hotel gardens look like a glittering golden carpet. One is almost cross with the sky for turning blue and yet more blue, but by daylight the view across the houses is also close to pure magic. With pointed roofs, small stair-wells, gazebos and many little turrets, the pavilions recall the typical "Lanna" architecture, the style of the "land of a million rice fields". The setting here is also, naturally, pre-programmed with its green-tinted rice terraces and gently curved hills – a brief glance is enough to touch the soul. The spa will also do you the world of good; thanks to its seven exclusive spa suites, the Four Seasons Resort Chiang Mai is famous for being one of the best in Thailand. This also applies to the restaurants, whose delicacies one can learn to prepare in the hotel's own cooking school. And should, by your endeavours, a touch too much salt land in the soup or the meat burn in the wok then do not worry, the evening brings consolation. Because the moment darkness falls over the hotel, the divine rain falls for a second time and everything turns gold.

Book to pack: "The King and I" by Margaret Landon

Four Seasons Resort Chiang Mai
Mae Rim-Samoeng Old Road
Mae Rim, Chiang Mai 50180, Thailand
Tel. +66 (53) 29 81 81
Fax +66 (53) 29 81 90
Website: www.fourseasons.com
www.great-escapes-hotels.com

DIRECTIONS	Situated in the heart of the valley of Mae Rim, 20 minutes north of Chiang Mai (airport transfer upon request).
RATES	$$$$
ROOMS	64 pavilion suites, 16 residence suites (these with personal "Mae Baan" or butler).
FOOD	Two restaurants with the finest Thai cooking and the "Elephant Bar" for drinks. The hotel has its own cooking school.
HISTORY	Opened in April 1995 and constructed in traditional Thai "Lanna" style.
X-FACTOR	Majestic – Relax like King of Siam himself.

Die Quelle des Lichts

Jeden Morgen lassen die Götter Goldstaub auf Chiang Mai regnen – wenn kurz vor der Dämmerung die Fackeln aufflackern, die Papyruslaternen sanft hin- und herschaukeln und die Windlichter einen zerbrechlichen Schein aussenden, sehen die Hotelgärten aus wie ein goldglitzernder Teppich. Man ist dem Himmel fast ein wenig böse, dass er blau und blauer wird; doch die Aussicht über die Häuser kommt auch bei Tageslicht reiner Magie ziemlich nahe. Mit spitz zulaufenden Dächern, kleinen Treppen, Erkern und ungezählten Türmchen erinnern die Pavillons an die typische »Lanna«-Architektur, den Stil des »Landes der Millionen Reisfelder«. Da ist natürlich auch die Kulisse vorprogrammiert: Grün schattierte Reisterrassen und sanft geschwungene Hügel – schon ein einziger Blick darauf streichelt die Seele. Ihr wird auch im Spa alles erdenklich Gute getan. Dank seiner sieben exklusiven Spa-Suiten ist das Four Seasons Resort Chiang Mai als eine der besten Wellness-Adressen Thailands berühmt. Das gilt auch für die Restaurants, deren Köstlichkeiten man in der hoteleigenen Cooking School nachkochen kann. Und sollte eine Prise Salz zu viel in der Suppe landen oder das Fleisch im Wok verkohlen, bringt der Abend Trost. Denn sobald sich die Dunkelheit über das Hotel legt, fällt ein zweites Mal der göttliche Regen – alles wird golden.
Buchtipp: »Der König und ich« von Margaret Landon

Aux sources de la lumière

Tous les matins, les dieux répandent une poudre d'or sur Chiang Mai. Lorsque juste avant l'aube les flambeaux se raniment une dernière fois, lorsque les lanternes en papyrus se balancent doucement et les chandelles jettent leur lueur tremblotante, les jardins des hôtels ressemblent à des tapis scintillants. On pourrait presque en vouloir au ciel de s'éclaircir inexorablement. Mais on se console bien vite car à la lumière du jour, la vue sur les toits des maisons est elle aussi magique. Avec leurs toits pointus, leurs petits escaliers, leurs encorbellements et leurs tours innombrables, les pavillons évoquent l'architecture « Lanna », le style caractéristique du pays aux mille rizières. Les collines aux formes arrondies et les rizières en terrasse déclinant leurs nuances de vert forment un décor qui ne peut que réjouir l'âme. Et celle-ci est particulièrement choyée dans ce centre de beauté et de remise en forme. Disposant de sept suites exclusives, le Four Seasons Resort Chiang Mai est l'une des meilleures adresses de Thaïlande. Cela vaut aussi pour ses restaurants dont vous pourrez apprendre les préparations exquises à la Cooking School de l'hôtel. Et si par mégarde vous avez salé un peu trop le potage ou laissé brûler la viande dans le wok, la tombée du jour vous fera oublier vos déboires, car dès que l'obscurité enveloppe l'hôtel, les dieux répandent leur poudre d'or une seconde fois.
Livre à emporter : « Le Roi et moi » de Margaret Landon

ANREISE	Mitten im Tal von Mae Rim gelegen, 20 Fahrtminuten nördlich von Chiang Mai (Flughafentransfer auf Wunsch).
PREIS	$$$$
ZIMMER	64 Pavilion-Suiten, 16 Residence-Suiten (mit persönlichem »Mae Baan«/Butler).
KÜCHE	2 Restaurants mit feinster thailändischer Küche, »Elephant Bar« für Drinks. Hoteleigene Kochschule.
GESCHICHTE	Eröffnet im April 1995 und im altthailändischen »Lanna«-Stil erbaut.
X-FAKTOR	Majestätisch – entspannen wie der König von Siam persönlich.

ACCÈS	Dans la vallée de Mae Rim, au nord de Chiang Mai, à 20 min de voiture (transfert par avion sur demande).
PRIX	$$$$
CHAMBRES	64 suites pavillon, 16 suites résidence (avec « Mae Baan »/majordôme individuel).
RESTAURATION	2 restaurants proposant une cuisine thaïlandaise raffinée, « Elephant Bar » pour les drinks. Ecole gastronomique appartenant à l'hôtel.
HISTOIRE	Ouvert en avril 1995 et construit dans le style traditionnel thaïlandais « Lanna ».
LE « PETIT PLUS »	Majestueux – se détendre comme le roi de Siam en personne.

Luxury Can Be This Simple...
La Résidence d'Angkor, Siem Reap

Luxury Can Be This Simple

Luxury can be that simple: A pool lined with 45 000 tiles – each reflecting a different shade of green – that has the same proportions as the artificial lakes of Cambodian temple complexes. A room with furniture made of local wood and bamboo, soft cotton materials and bright, colourful pillows. And a balcony that seems custom-made for a private breakfast or a game of draughts. La Résidence d'Angkor, situated on the river in the heart of Siem Reap and just a short walk from Angkor Wat, does not let itself be intimidated by the grandeur of its environment and shows its own version of Cambodia – a quiet, warm-hearted and obliging country. In the building itself, materials and skills from other lands only play tiny, minor roles; the predominant wood, bamboo, stone and fabrics come from the immediate vicinity and are processed in local workshops as well as in workshops for the disabled. Food is cooked according to traditional recipes and with fresh ingredients; used water is not just poured into the ground but used to irrigate the garden; you don't cruise around the neighbourhood in a car but ride a bicycle. It sounds a bit like eco-tourism and Spartan living – but is worlds away from that, because, like we said: Luxury really can be this simple.

Book to pack: "The Royal Way" by André Malraux

La Résidence d'Angkor	
River Road	
Siem Reap, Cambodia	
Tel. +855 (63) 96 33 90	
Fax +855 (63) 96 33 91	
Email: reservations@residencedangkor.com	
Website: www.residencedangkor.com	
www.great-escapes-hotels.com	

DIRECTIONS	Situated in the centre of Siem Reap, 7 km/4 miles southeast of the airport and 10 minutes from the temple grounds.
RATES	$$
ROOMS	54 rooms and 1 suite.
FOOD	Traditional Asian specialities, French Haute Cuisine with Khmer flavors, as well as snacks in the bar with a beautiful view of the river.
HISTORY	Opened in February 2002.
X-FACTOR	Khmer flair and the comfort of modern Cambodia.

So schlicht kann Luxus sein

Ein Pool, der mit 45 000 Kacheln ausgelegt ist, von denen jede in einem anderen Grünton schimmert, und der denselben Proportionen besitzt wie die künstlichen Seen kambodschanischer Tempelanlagen. Ein Zimmer mit Möbeln aus einheimischem Holz und Bambus, weichen Baumwollstoffen und leuchtend bunte Kissen. Ein Balkon wie geschaffen für ein privates Frühstück oder eine Partie Dame. Das Hotel La Résidence d'Angkor, am Fluss mitten in Siem Reap gelegen und nur einen Spaziergang von Angkor Wat entfernt, lässt sich von der Grandezza seiner Umgebung nicht einschüchtern und zeigt sein eigenes Kambodscha – ein ruhiges, warmherziges und zuvorkommendes Land. Materialien und Fähigkeiten aus fremden Nationen sollten beim Bau nur winzige Nebenrollen spielen; Holz, Bambus, Stein und Stoffe stammen aus der unmittelbaren Umgebung und wurden in lokalen Handwerksbetrieben und Behindertenwerkstätten verarbeitet. Gekocht wird nach überlieferten Rezepten aus frischen Zutaten, einmal verwendetes Wasser versickert nicht nutzlos im Boden, sondern dient zur Gartenbewässerung. Man rollt nicht ständig mit dem Auto durch die Gegend, sondern setzt sich aufs Fahrrad. Es klingt ein wenig nach Ökotourismus und mangelndem Komfort – und ist doch Welten davon entfernt. Denn wie gesagt: So schlicht kann Luxus sein.

Buchtipp: »Der Königsweg« von André Malraux

Le luxe est dans la sobriété

Une piscine aux innombrables carreaux dont chacun jette des lueurs d'un vert différent et qui présente les mêmes proportions que les lacs artificiels des temples cambodgiens. Une chambre aux meubles en bois et en bambou décorée de douces étoffes en coton et de coussins aux couleurs vives. Un balcon qui donne envie de prendre le petit-déjeuner en tête à tête ou de faire une partie de dames. La Résidence d'Angkor, situé près du fleuve en plein cœur de Siem Reap et à quelques kilomètres d'Angkor Wat, ne se laisse pas intimider par le décor grandiose et montre son propre Cambodge – un pays tranquille où les habitants sont accueillants et pleins d'attentions. Lors de la construction de l'hôtel, les matériaux et le savoir-faire étrangers n'ont joué qu'un petit rôle. Le bois, le bambou, la pierre et les étoffes proviennent des environs et ont été travaillés dans les entreprises artisanales et les centres pour handicapés de la région. La cuisine est préparée avec des produits frais selon des recettes traditionnelles. Les eaux usées ne sont pas jetées inconsidérément mais servent à arroser le jardin, on enfourche son vélo pour sillonner les environs au lieu de prendre constamment la voiture. Tout cela peut donner l'impression d'un tourisme écologique et d'un manque de confort, mais ce n'est absolument pas le cas, car le véritable luxe est dans la simplicité des choses.

Livre à emporter : « La Voie royale » d'André Malraux

ANREISE	Im Zentrum von Siem Reap gelegen, 7 km südöstlich des Flughafens und zehn Minuten von den Tempelanlagen entfernt.
PREIS	$$
ZIMMER	54 Zimmer und 1 Suite.
KÜCHE	Traditionelle asiatische Spezialitäten und französische Haute Cuisine mit Khmer-Aromen. Außerdem Snacks in der Bar mit traumhaftem Flussblick.
GESCHICHTE	Im Februar 2002 eröffnet.
X-FAKTOR	Khmer-Flair und der Komfort des modernen Kambodscha.

ACCÈS	Situé dans le centre de Siem Reap à 7 km au sud-est de l'aéroport et à 10 min des temples.
PRIX	$$
CHAMBRES	54 chambres et 1 suite.
RESTAURATION	Spécialités asiatiques traditionnelles et Haute Cuisine française aux arômes Khmer. Le bar propose des snacks et une vue magnifique sur le fleuve.
HISTOIRE	Ouvert en février 2002.
LE « PETIT PLUS »	Allie ambiance khmère et confort du Cambodge moderne.

A Blue Break...
Cheong Fatt Tze Mansion, Penang

A Blue Break

In Asia there are also careers which lead from dishwasher
to millionaire: When Cheong Fatt Tze left his hometown in
1856 aged 16, he did so without a penny in his purse and
only a few decades later he was one of the richest men in
the world. He presided over railroad and banking businesses
and in economic circles was referred to as "China's last mandarin and first capitalist" or "the Rockefeller of the East".
In between his travels throughout Asia, he always returned
to Malaysia, to his house in Penang, which even then was
considered to be one of the city's most beautiful buildings.
After a complete renovation in 1990, it received an award
from Unesco and lent colour to the movie "Indochina" with
Catherine Deneuve. Today it is a hotel that connects the
myth and magic of China with the splendour and glory of
the British Empire. The Cheong Fatt Tze Mansion – which
thanks to its bright indigo facade is also called the Blue
Mansion – has preserved the style of the late nineteenth
century. Filigree Chinese woodcarvings, Scottish lamps, cur-
tains of handwoven gauze and silk, mouth-blown glass and
fine porcelain adorn the 16 individually furnished rooms. If
you sit in one of the five inner courtyards, stroll through the
garden or try to count the 220 small windows, you are trans-
ported back to the history of the Blue Mansion and reminded
of the great career of Cheong Fatt Tze.

Book to pack: "Malaysia. Heart of Southeast Asia"
by Gavin Young

Cheong Fatt Tze Mansion	
14 Leith Street	
10200, Penang, Malaysia	
Tel. +60 (4) 262 00 06	
Fax +60 (4) 262 52 89	
Email: cftm@tm.net.my	
Website: www.cheongfatttzemansion.com	
www.great-escapes-hotels.com	

DIRECTIONS	Situated in the historical centre of Penang, 30–45 minutes from Penang Airport.
RATES	$
ROOMS	16 individually furnished double rooms in the style of the late nineteenth century.
FOOD	Breakfast in the pretty alfresco area of an inner courtyard, afternoon tea and drinks as well (bar with a wine cellar).
HISTORY	The former house of Cheong Fatt Tze has been turned into one of the most beautiful Chinese-inspired courtyard houses.
X-FACTOR	A high point in handcrafted art.

Eine blaue Pause

Auch in Asien gibt es Karrieren, die vom Tellerwäscher zum Millionär führen: Als Cheong Fatt Tze 1856 mit 16 Jahren seine Heimatstadt verließ, tat er es ohne eine Münze in der Tasche – und nur wenige Jahrzehnte später war er einer der reichsten Männer der Welt, stand Eisenbahnunternehmen sowie Banken vor und wurde in wirtschaftspolitischen Kreisen nur noch »Chinas letzter Mandarin und erster Kapitalist« oder »Rockefeller des Ostens« genannt. Zwischen seinen Reisen durch ganz Asien kam er immer wieder nach Malaysia, in sein Haus in Penang, das schon damals zu den schönsten Gebäuden der Stadt zählte. Nach einer Rundumrenovierung 1990 wurde es von der Unesco preisgekrönt und verlieh dem Kinofilm »Indochine« mit Catherine Deneuve Farbe – heute ist es ein Hotel, das Mythos und Magie Chinas mit Glanz und Glorie des Britischen Empire verbindet. Die Cheong Fatt Tze Mansion, die dank ihrer Fassade in leuchtendem Indigo auch als Blue Mansion bekannt ist, hat sich den Stil des späten 19. Jahrhunderts bewahrt. Die 16 individuell eingerichteten Zimmer schmücken filigrane chinesische Holzschnitzereien, schottische Lampen, Vorhänge aus handgewebtem Gaze und Seide, mundgeblasenes Glas und feines Porzellan. Wer in einem der fünf Innenhöfe sitzt, durch den Garten schlendert oder versucht, die 220 kleinen Fenster zu zählen, wird in die Geschichte der Blue Mansion zurückversetzt und an die große Karriere des Cheong Fatt Tze erinnert.

Buchtipp: »Sternenhimmel über Malaysia« von Marion Nikola

La maison bleue

En Asie, un cireur de chaussures peut aussi devenir millionnaire. Un jour de 1856, Cheong Fatt Tze, âgé de seize ans, quitta sa ville natale sans un sou en poche. Quelques dizaines d'années plus tard, il était l'un des hommes les plus riches du monde. Propriétaire de banques et de chemins de fer, on le surnommait dans les milieux économiques et politiques « le dernier mandarin de Chine et le premier capitaliste » ou encore « le Rockefeller de l'Orient ». Entre ses nombreux voyages à travers l'Asie, il revenait toujours en Malaisie dans sa maison de Penang, jadis des plus beaux bâtiments de la ville. Après une rénovation complète en 1990, elle fut primée par l'Unesco et on peut l'admirer dans le film « Indochine » avec Catherine Deneuve. Aujourd'hui cette maison est un hôtel qui marie les mythes et la magie de la Chine avec la splendeur et la gloire de l'Empire britannique. La Cheong Fatt Tze Mansion qui, en raison de sa façade bleu indigo, est aussi connue sous le nom de Blue Mansion a conservé le style de la fin du 19e siècle. Les 16 chambres, aménagées de façon individuelle, sont décorées avec de filigranes sculptures en bois chinoises, des lampes écossaises, des rideaux en gaze et en soie, tissés à la main, du verre soufflé à l'ancienne et de la porcelaine fine. Le visiteur qui s'assoit dans l'une des cinq cours intérieures, se promène dans le jardin ou essaie de compter les multiples petites fenêtres (220 en tout !), se retrouve transporté dans le passé de la Blue Mansion et pense bien sûr à la grande carrière de Cheong Fatt Tze.

Livre à emporter : « Malaisie, cœur de l'Asie du Sud-Est » de Gavin Young

ANREISE	Im historischen Zentrum von Penang gelegen, 30 bis 45 Fahrtminuten vom Flughafen Penang entfernt.	ACCÈS	Situé dans le centre historique de Penang, à 30–45 min en voiture de l'aéroport de Penang.
PREIS	$	PRIX	$
ZIMMER	16 individuell eingerichtete Doppelzimmer im Stil des späten 19. Jahrhunderts.	CHAMBRES	16 chambres doubles aménagées individuellement dans le style de la fin du 19e siècle.
KÜCHE	Frühstück in einem Innenhof, außerdem Afternoon-Tea und Drinks (Bar mit Weinkeller).	RESTAURATION	Petit-déjeuner dans une cour intérieure. Thé de cinq heures et boissons (bar doté d'une cave à vins).
GESCHICHTE	Aus dem ehemaligen Haus von Cheong Fatt Tze wurde eines der schönsten chinesisch inspirierten Courtyard-Houses.	HISTOIRE	L'ancienne maison de Cheong Fatt Tze est devenue l'une des plus belles courtyard-houses d'inspiration chinoise.
X-FAKTOR	Ein Höhepunkt der Handwerkskunst.	LE « PETIT PLUS »	L'artisanat d'art à son apogée.

Tropical Magic...
The Datai, Langkawi

Tropical Magic

God must have personally placed this island in the ocean
after he had finished with the rest of the world – carefully,
like a floating candle, after having touched up the rainforest
again with a gentle brush. Ever since, Langkawi has lain
like a pearl before Malaysia's west coast – with beaches too
beautiful for any advertisement. The tropical heat is forgot-
ten at the sight of the green-mantled hills and waterfalls.
Wouldn't it be wonderful to own a house here, to stroll during the day along winding paths through the jungle and in
the evening to watch the setting sun illuminate the Andaman Sea? Well, The Datai makes it possible, if not for a whole
lifetime, then for a whole holiday at least. On slopes leading
down to the icing sugar beach, there are villas linked by a
labyrinth of paths, decked with cool stone or such shiny polished wood that they could easily pass for a mirror. Natural
beige and brown tones and clear lines determine the design
of the rooms – in the correct understanding that more splendour and glamour would have been a futile attempt to compete with mother nature outside the door. Dashes of colour
are only allowed in "Mandara Spa" where you can lie in bath-
tubs filled with colourful flowers and look out across *God's
own country*.

Book to pack: "Love and Vertigo" by Hsu-Ming Teo

The Datai	
Jalan Teluk Datai,	
07000 Pulau Langkawi	
Kedah Darul Aman, Malaysia	
Tel. +60 (4) 959 25 00	
Fax +60 (4) 959 26 00	
Email: datai@ghmhotels.com	
Website: www.ghmhotels.com	
www.great-escapes-hotels.com	

DIRECTIONS	Situated on the northwest coast of Langkawi, a 30-minute drive from the airport (the transfer is organized).
RATES	$$$$
ROOMS	54 deluxe rooms, 40 villas, 18 suites.
FOOD	Malaysian, Thai and western specialities, most beautifully at the open-air restaurant "The Pavilion" or in "The Beach Club" directly on the beach.
HISTORY	Opened in 1994.
X-FACTOR	A paradise – thankfully without apple trees.

Tropischer Zauber

Diese Insel muss Gott persönlich ins Meer gesetzt haben, als er mit dem Rest der Welt fertig war – vorsichtig wie eine Schwimmkerze und erst, nachdem er den Regenwald mit einem weichen Pinsel noch einmal abgestaubt hatte. Seither liegt Langkawi perlengleich vor Malaysias Westküste; mit Stränden zu schön für jeden Werbespot, grün überzogenen Hügeln und mit Wasserfällen, bei deren Anblick man alle Tropenhitze vergisst. Wäre es nicht wunderbar, hier ein Haus zu besitzen, tagsüber auf gewundenen Pfaden durch den Dschungel zu spazieren und abends zu sehen, wie die untergehende Sonne die Andamanische See aufglühen lässt? Wenn nicht für ein ganzes Leben – für einen ganzen Urlaub macht The Datai das möglich. An Hängen und bis zum Puderzuckerstrand hinunter stehen Villen, die ein Labyrinth von Wegen verbindet; ausgelegt mit kühlem Stein oder so blank poliertem Holz, dass es ohne weiteres als Spiegel durchgehen könnte. Beige und braune Naturtöne und klare Linien bestimmen das Design der Zimmer – im richtigen Bewusstsein, dass mehr Glanz und Glamour ein vergeblicher Versuch gewesen wären, mit der Natur draußen vor der Tür zu konkurrieren. Farbtupfer sind nur im »Mandara Spa« erlaubt, wo man in mit bunten Blüten gefüllten Badewannen liegt und hinausblickt auf *gods own country*.
Buchtipp: »Jadetöchter« von Hsu-Ming Teo

Des Tropiques de rêve

Dieu lui-même a dû créer cette île après s'être accordé un repos bien mérité – il l'a posée avec précaution sur les flots, ayant pris soin d'épousseter la forêt vierge avec un doux pinceau. Depuis, Langkawi repose telle une perle devant la côte ouest de la Malaisie. Ses plages sont trop belles pour les spots publicitaires, ses collines verdoyantes et ses cascades font oublier les températures tropicales.
Ne serait-il pas merveilleux de posséder une maison ici, d'explorer durant la journée les chemins sinueux qui traversent la jungle et de regarder le soir le soleil embraser le lac Andamini ? The Datai peut exaucer ce rêve – au moins le temps des vacances. Sur les pentes des collines et jusqu'à la plage de sable fin se dressent des villas que relie un labyrinthe de chemins. Elles sont en pierre ou en bois si poli que l'on pourrait s'y mirer. Des tons naturels beige et ocre et des lignes claires déterminent le design des pièces. Les aménager avec plus d'éclat et de glamour ne serait en effet qu'une vaine tentative d'entrer en compétition avec la nature environnante.
Des accents de couleur ne sont autorisés qu'au « Mandara Spa ». Ici, on peut s'allonger dans des baignoires où flottent des fleurs multicolores et regarder au dehors « gods own country ».
Livre à emporter : « Salina » d'Abdul Samad Said

ANREISE	An der Nordwestküste von Langkawi gelegen, 30 Fahrtminuten vom Flughafen entfernt (Transfer wird organisiert).	ACCÈS	Situé sur la côte nord-ouest de l'île de Langkawi, à 30 min de voiture de l'aéroport (le transfert est organisé).
PREIS	$$$$	PRIX	$$$$
ZIMMER	54 Deluxe-Zimmer, 40 Villen, 18 Suiten.	CHAMBRES	54 chambres de luxe, 40 villas, 18 suites.
KÜCHE	Malaysische, thailändische und westliche Spezialitäten, am schönsten im Open-air-Restaurant »The Pavillion« oder im »The Beach Club« direkt am Strand.	RESTAURATION	Spécialités malaisiennes, thai et occidentales, le plus beau cadre est le restaurant en plein air « The Pavillion » ou « The Beach Club » sur la plage.
GESCHICHTE	1994 eröffnet.	HISTOIRE	Ouvert en 1994.
X-FAKTOR	Ein Paradies – zum Glück ohne Apfelbäume.	LE « PETIT PLUS »	Un paradis – mais ne cherchez pas le pommier.

The Blue Hour...
Banyan Tree Spa Bintan, Bintan Island

Banyan Tree Spa Bintan, Bintan Island

The Blue Hour

Singapore was once closer to the tropics than any other city. You were almost completely surrounded by greenery; your skin was lightly coated with a film of moisture and you could hear the birds singing and smell the rain long before it drummed on the ground. Today Singapore primarily tends to keep the tropics at a distance: With houses whose air conditioning systems generate an ice age regardless of the real climate outside. Windows can no longer be opened and shopping centres are always sealed in glass – there are days when you only move in the artificial world between underground car park, office, supermarket and apartment, never once encountering a single breath of fresh air. But not to worry, if you are missing contact with nature then you don't have to look far. A 45-minute crossing from Singapore to Bintan Island should do the trick, because here the Banyan Tree Spa brings back all the long-forgotten charm of the region to Bintan. Villas stand on the outskirts of the jungle and by the ocean like little packages of paradise. They are sparingly designed with a limited palette and clear lines, but each features a personal touch lent by a bright blossom in a glass, a patterned pillow or an unusual stone on the shelf. One villa serves as a private spa and has all of the splendours of Asia in oil and cream form. Others are truly *on the rocks*, balancing high above the sea, and yet more are to be found completely encircled by forest. A promise: This is a place to rediscover the tropics – and oneself at the same time.

Book to pack: "Sinister Twilight. The fall of Singapore "
by Noel Barber

Banyan Tree Spa Bintan	
Jalan Teluk Berembang	
Laguna Bintan, Bintan Resorts	
Logoi 29155, Indonesia	
Tel. +62 (770) 69 31 00	
Fax +62 (770) 69 32 00	
Email: reservations@banyantree.com;	
spa-bintan@banyantree.com	
Website: www.banyantree.com	
www.great-escapes-hotels.com	

DIRECTIONS	Situated on the northwest point of Bintan Island, southeast of Singapore (45-minute crossing in a high-speed catamaran).
RATES	$$$$
ROOMS	55 Jacuzzi villas, 6 sea-view pool villas, 8 bay front pool villas, 1 spa pool villa.
FOOD	Southeast Asian cuisine in the "Saffron" and Mediterranean food in "The Cove".
HISTORY	Opened in 1995.
X-FACTOR	A sigh of relief in old Asia.

Blaue Stunde

Singapur war einst den Tropen so nah wie kaum eine zweite
Stadt. Man saß fast überall im Grünen, hatte einen leichten
Feuchtigkeitsfilm auf der Haut, hörte die Vögel singen und
roch den Regen, lange bevor er auf die Erde prasselte. Heute
hält Singapur die Tropen meist auf Distanz: Mit Häusern, in
denen Klimaanlagen ohne Rücksicht aufs Wetter eine Eiszeit
produzieren, mit Fenstern, die sich nicht mehr öffnen lassen,
und rundum verglasten Einkaufszentren – es gibt Tage, an
denen man auf frische Luft verzichtet und sich nur in der
künstlichen Welt zwischen Tiefgarage, Büro, Supermarkt
und Apartment bewegen kann. Doch keine Sorge: Wer das
Naturgefühl vermisst, braucht nicht lange zu suchen. Eine
45-minütige Überfahrt von Singapur zur Insel Bintan genügt, denn dort verströmt das Banyan Tree Spa Bintan all
den vergessen geglaubten Charme der Region. Am Rand des
Dschungels und am Ozean stehen Villen wie kleine Paradiese; mit wenigen Farben und klaren Linien sparsam designt
und zugleich mit persönlichem Touch – dank einer leuchten-
den Blüte im Glas, einem gemusterten Kissen oder einem
seltenen Stein auf dem Regal. Es gibt eine Villa, die zugleich
als privates Spa dient und alle Herrlichkeiten Asiens in Öl-
und Cremeform besitzt, andere Häuser, die *on the rocks* hoch
über dem Meer balancieren, und dritte, die auf allen Seiten
von Wald umschlossen sind. Es ist ein Versprechen: Hier
findet man die Tropen wieder – und sich selbst noch dazu.
Buchtipp: »Tanamera. Der Roman Singapurs« von Noel Barber

L'heure bleue

Singapour a probablement été autrefois plus proche des
Tropiques qu'aucune autre ville. La végétation était quasi
omniprésente, l'humidité ambiante recouvrait la peau d'un
léger voile de sueur, les oiseaux chantaient et on sentait la
pluie bien avant que l'averse n'arrive.

Aujourd'hui, Singapour aurait plutôt tendance à tenir les
Tropiques à distance, avec des maisons climatisées sans
souci des températures environnantes, des fenêtres hermé-
tiquement closes et des centres d'achats sous verre – on peut
se déplacer dans ce monde artificiel entre le parking souter-
rain, le bureau, le supermarché et l'appartement sans jamais
se rendre à l'air libre.

Mais les amoureux de la nature ne doivent pas chercher
longtemps. Situé à trois quarts d'heures de bateau de Singapour, sur l'île Bintan, le Banyan Tree Spa Bintan émane tout
ce charme que l'on croyait oublié. A l'orée de la jungle et au
bord de la mer de Chine, se dressent des villas paradisiaques
aux teintes sobres et aux lignes simples et claires, avec en
même temps une touche personnelle – une fleur éclatante
dans un vase, un coussin aux beaux motifs ou une pierre
rare sur une étagère.

Une villa fait office de centre de remise en forme privé et
possède ce que l'Asie a de meilleur sous forme d'onguents
et d'huiles, d'autres maisons sont posées en équilibre sur
les falaises qui surplombent la mer, et d'autres encore sont
entourées de végétation luxuriante. Ici, on retrouve les Tropiques – et en plus, on se retrouve soi-même.
**Livres à emporter : « La vie n'est pas une foire nocturne »
de Pramoedya Anata Toer**
« L'étreinte de Singapour » de J. G. Farrell

ANREISE	An der nordwestlichen Spitze der Insel Bintan gelegen, südöstlich von Singapur (45-minütige Überfahrt im High-speed-Katamaran).
PREIS	$$$$
ZIMMER	55 Jacuzzi-Villen, 6 Seaview-Pool-Villen, 8 Bayfront-Pool-Villen, 1 Spa-Pool-Villa.
KÜCHE	Südostasiatisches im Restaurant »Saffron«, Mediterranes im »The Cove«.
GESCHICHTE	1995 eröffnet.
X-FAKTOR	Aufatmen im alten Asien.

ACCÈS	Situé au nord-ouest de la pointe de l'île Bintan, au sud-est de Singapour (traversée en 45 min dans un catamaran à grande vitesse).
PRIX	$$$$
CHAMBRES	55 Jacuzzi Villas, 6 Seaview Pool Villas, 8 Bayfront Pool Villas, 1 Spa Pool Villa.
RESTAURATION	Extrême-orientale au « Saffron », méridionale à « The Cove ».
HISTOIRE	Ouvert en 1995
LE « PETIT PLUS »	Un grand moment de détente dans l'Asie ancienne.

A Building for Buddha...
Amanjiwo, Java

Amanjiwo, Java

A Building for Buddha

Ten thousand craftsmen slaved away for almost an entire century, dragging stone after stone, shaping and piling them on top of one another – and when the Temple of Borobudur was complete, Merapi Volcano erupted and buried the lot under lava and ashes. But the legend of Borobudur lived on, and excavations began at the start of the nineteenth century. Thirty years ago, Unesco supported the complete restoration of the temple and today Borobudur is again the largest and perhaps most beautiful temple complex in southeast Asia. The architecture of Amanjiwo was influenced by its splendour – it reflects ideas and details of the complex, radiates the same solemnity and peace, and when one looks across the rice fields, one looks directly at Borobudur itself. Opened several years ago, Amanjiwo simply seems to have merged with the nature of Central Java. The light "paras yogya" limestone stems from the region and assumes the colour of the tree trunks. The green, brown and cream tones of the forest and earth can also be found on pillow cases and bedspreads, and the pale wash of blue sky over the island gives the pool its own unique shimmer. If you stay in one of the suites with the cool terrazzo floor and high ceilings, you experience the classic, elegant style of Java with light accents on dark wood, rattan furniture and traditional glass painting. The "normal" windows present a view of your choice, either the hills, the farmland or Borobudur – inspiration in its purest form.

Book to pack: "Child of All Nations" by Pramoedya Ananta Toer

Amanjiwo	
Borobudur, Java, Indonesia	
Tel. +62 (293) 78 83 33	
Fax +62 (293) 78 83 55	
Email: reservations@amanresorts.com	
Website: www.amanresorts.com	
www.great-escapes-hotels.com	

DIRECTIONS	Situated in Central Java, 1.5 hr. northwest of Yogyakarta Airport and 2 hr. southwest of Solo Airport.
RATES	$$$$
ROOMS	36 suites, including 5 pool suites, 10 deluxe pool suites and 1 Dalem Jiwo Suite.
FOOD	Indonesian specialities.
HISTORY	Opened in 1997 and designed to mirror the holiness of the Borobudur Temple.
X-FACTOR	Buddha was never so close.

Ein Bauwerk für den Buddha

Fast ein ganzes Jahrhundert hatten sich insgesamt 10 000
Handwerker abgemüht, hatten Steine herangeschleppt,
in Form gebracht und aufeinandergetürmt – und als der
Tempel von Borobudur vollendet war, brach der Vulkan
Merapi aus und begrub ihn unter Lava und Asche. Doch die
Legende von Borobudur lebte fort, zu Beginn des 19. Jahrhunderts begannen die Ausgrabungen, vor dreißig Jahren
unterstützte die UNESCO eine umfassende Sanierung und
heute präsentiert sich Borobudur wieder als größter und
vielleicht schönster Tempelkomplex Südostasiens. Von seinem Glanz ließ sich die Architektur von Amanjiwo beein-
flussen – sie spiegelt Ideen und Details der Anlage wieder,
strahlt dieselbe Erhabenheit und Ruhe aus, und wenn man
über die Reisfelder blickt, blickt man direkt auf Borobudur
selbst. Vor einigen Jahren eröffnet, scheint Amanjiwo schon
wie selbstverständlich mit der Natur Zentraljavas verwachsen zu sein. Der helle Kalkstein »paras yogya« stammt aus
der Region und nimmt die Farbe der Baumstämme auf; die
Grün-, Braun- und Cremetöne von Wald und Erde entdeckt
man auch auf Kissenbezügen und Tagesdecken, und der ver-
waschen blaue Himmel über der Insel verleiht den Pools
ihren ganz eigenen Schimmer. Wer in einer der Suiten mit
kühlem Terrazzoboden und hohen Decken wohnt, erlebt den
klassisch-eleganten Stil Javas; mit hellen Akzenten auf dunklem Holz, Rattanmöbeln und traditionellen Glasmalereien.
Die »normalen« Fenster zeigen im übrigen ganz nach
Wunsch auf die Hügel, das Farmland oder Borobudur –
Inspiration in ihrer reinsten Form.
Buchtipp: »Kind aller Völker« von Pramoedya Ananta Toer

Une construction pour Bouddha

Pendant près d'un siècle, les dix milles artisans s'étaient
tués à la tâche, ils avaient apporté péniblement les pierres
sur le site, les avaient taillées, puis les avaient amoncelées –
et lorsque le temple de Borobudur fut achevé, le volcan
Merapi se réveilla et l'ensevelit sous la lave et les cendres.
Pourtant la légende continua de vivre, au 19e siècle des
fouilles furent entreprises et, il y a trente ans, l'UNESCO
mit des fonds à disposition en vue d'une restauration complète. Aujourd'hui, Borobudur est le complexe le plus grand,
et peut-être le plus beau, de toute l'Asie du Sud-Est. Son
éclat a inspiré l'architecture d'Amanjiwo, qui reflète les idées
et les détails du temple, dégage la même sérénité et lorsque
le regard glisse au-dessus des rizières, il tombe directement
sur Borobudur. Ouvert depuis quelques années, Amanjiwo
semble s'être intégré tout naturellement au paysage du
centre de Java. La pierre calcaire de couleur claire, appelée
ici « paras yogya », provient des environs et absorbe la
couleur des troncs d'arbre ; les tons de vert, de marron et de
crème de la forêt réapparaissent sur les coussins et les
nappes, et le bleu délavé du ciel confère aux piscines une
brillance qui n'existe nulle part ailleurs. Le client qui séjour-
ne dans l'une des suites au sol en terre cuite et au plafond
élevé peut voir dans toute sa splendeur le style classique et
élégant de Java avec ses accents clairs sur les bois sombres,
ses meubles en osier et ses peintures sur verre traditionnelles. Suivant les préférences de l'hôte, les fenêtres « nor-
males » de sa chambre donnent sur les collines, les fermes
ou Borobudur – l'inspiration sous sa forme la plus pure.
Livre à emporter : « Le Monde des hommes »
de Pramoedya Ananta Toer

ANREISE	In Zentraljava gelegen, 1,5h nordwestlich vom Flughafen Yogyakarta und 2h südwestlich vom Flughafen Solo.
PREIS	$$$$
ZIMMER	36 Suiten, darunter 5 Pool-Suiten und 10 Deluxe-Pool-Suiten und 1 Dalem-Jiwo-Suite.
KÜCHE	Indonesische Spezialitäten.
GESCHICHTE	1997 eröffnet und wie ein Spiegelbild des Heiligtums Borobudur gestaltet.
X-FAKTOR	Noch nie war Buddha so nah.

ACCÈS	Situé dans le centre de Java à 1 h ½ au nord-ouest de l'aéroport de Yogyakarta et à 2 h au sud-ouest de l'aéroport de Solo.
PRIX	$$$$
CHAMBRES	36 suites, dont 5 suites avec piscine, 10 suites de luxe avec piscine et 1 suite Dalem Jiwo.
RESTAURATION	Spécialités indonésiennes.
HISTOIRE	Ouvert en 1997 et décoré comme un miroir du lieu saint de Borobudur.
LE « PETIT PLUS »	Bouddha n'a jamais été aussi proche.

A Cupful of Happiness...
Losari Coffee Plantation – Resort and Spa, Java

Losari Coffee Plantation – Resort and Spa, Java

A Cupful of Happiness

The rising sun casts a veil of light over the treetops; the volcanoes stand on the horizon like silent guards. The air is filled with the fragrance of fruit and spices – and of coffee: Of fresh roasted and ground beans, so intense that you feel wide awake from the scent alone. The brown-black gold is grown and processed right in front of the house door on the Losari Coffee Plantation in the highlands of central Java.

As in times long past, coffee beans are cultivated and harvested here (more than 25 tons per year) and so are bananas, peanuts, coconuts, cloves, ginger and cinnamon. It is only recently that guests have also had the opportunity to experience this huge open-air museum, because Losari is now a plantation, luxury lodge and spa in one. The former farmhouse dating from 1928 has been turned into a colonial-style reception area with lounge, library and a veranda with a view of the sunset that is to die for. The villas have the charm of old Java – many of them taken from ancient villages and rebuilt here in all their original detail. In the midst of the tropical vegetation, Gabriella Teggia also placed a Turkish hammam, which washes away all of the soul's worries and stress. Here the Italian owner, who previously co-founded the Hotel Amandari on Bali, unifies the most diverse cultures and with Losari has built one of Asia's most beautiful resorts and certainly the most fragrant.

Book to pack: "Max Havelaar or The Coffee Sales Of The Netherlands" by Multatuli

Losari Coffee Plantation – Resort and Spa
P. O. Box 108
Magelang 56100
Central Java, Indonesia
Tel. +62 (298) 59 63 33
Fax +62 (298) 59 26 96
Website: www.losari.info
www.great-escapes-hotels.com

DIRECTIONS	Situated in the highlands of central Java (900 m), 60 km/ 37 miles from Yogyakarta and 45 km/28 miles from both Semarang and Solo.
RATES	$$$
ROOMS	7 villas, 3 bungalows, 7 suites, 1 Villa Bella Vista with five bedrooms.
FOOD	"Java Red" with Mediterranean-inspired cuisine, "Java Green" with light dishes.
HISTORY	Former Dutch coffee plantation founded in 2003.
X-FACTOR	This is what Java tastes like!

Eine Tasse voll Glück

Die aufgehende Sonne legt einen Schleier aus Licht über die Baumkronen, am Horizont stehen die Vulkane wie stumme Wächter, in der Luft liegt ein Duft nach Obst und Gewürzen. Und nach Kaffee – nach frisch gerösteten und gemahlenen Bohnen; so intensiv, dass man allein vom Riechen hellwach wird. Angebaut und verarbeitet wird das braunschwarze Gold direkt vor der Haustür: auf der Losari Coffee Plantation im Hochland Zentraljavas. Wie in längst vergangenen Zeiten kultiviert und erntet man hier Kaffeebohnen (mehr als 25 Tonnen sind es pro Jahr), außerdem Bananen, Erd- und Kokosnüsse, Nelken, Ingwer und Zimt. Seit kurzem erst haben Gäste die Möglichkeit, dieses überdimensionale Freilichtmuseum zu erleben – denn Losari ist Plantage, Luxus-Lodge und Spa in einem. Aus dem ehemaligen Farmhaus von 1928 wurde ein Empfangsbereich im Kolonialstil mit Lounge, Bibliothek und einer Veranda, von der aus der Blick in den Sonnenuntergang zum Dahinschmelzen schön ist. Die Villen besitzen den Charme des alten Java – viele von ihnen wurden in ursprünglichen Dörfern ab- und hier detailgetreu wieder aufgebaut. Mitten in die tropische Vegetation ließ Gabriella Teggia auch einen türkischen Hammam stellen, in dem alle Sorgen und aller Stress von der Seele gewaschen werden. Die Italienerin, die bereits das Hotel Amandari auf Bali mitbegründete, macht hier aus unterschiedlichsten Kulturen eine Einheit und hat mit Losari eines der schönsten Resorts Asiens geschaffen – und mit Sicherheit das duftendste.

Buchtipp: »Max Havelaar oder Die Kaffeeversteigerung der Niederländischen Handelsgesellschaft« von Multatuli

Une tasse de bonheur

Le soleil levant baigne de lumière la cime des arbres, à l'horizon les volcans se dressent comme d'impassibles gardiens, l'air embaume les fruits et les épices. Mais l'on perçoit aussi une délicieuse odeur de café fraîchement moulu, une odeur si intense qu'elle suffit à vous éveiller complètement. Le café est cultivé et torréfié juste en face de la maison, sur la plantation de café Losari. Comme dans le passé, on cultive ici, sur les hauts plateaux du centre de Java, du café (plus de vingt-cinq tonnes par an), des bananes, des cacahuètes, des noix de coco, des clous de girofle, du gingembre et de la cannelle. Depuis peu les clients ont la possibilité de visiter cette immense musée en plein air – car Losari est à la fois une plantation, un lodge de luxe et un centre de remise en forme. L'ancienne ferme, datant de 1928, a été transformée en une salle de réception de style colonial, qui comprend un salon, une bibliothèque et une véranda d'où l'on peut contempler un coucher du soleil de toute beauté. Les villas possèdent le charme de l'ancienne Java et beaucoup d'entre elles furent démontées dans les villages pour être reconstruites ici en respectant tous les détails. Au milieu de cette végétation tropicale, Gabriella Teggia a aussi fait installer un hammam qui vous fait oublier stress et soucis. L'Italienne, cofondatrice de l'hôtel Amandari à Bali, marie avec bonheur diverses cultures. Avec Losari, elle a créé l'un des plus beaux resorts de toute l'Asie – et certainement le plus odorant.

Livre à emporter : « Max Havelaar ou les ventes de café de la compagnie commerciale des Pays-Bas » de Multatuli

ANREISE	Im Hochland von Zentraljava gelegen (900 m), 60 km von Yogyakarta und je 45 km von Semarang und Solo entfernt.	ACCÈS	A 60 km de Yogyakarta et à 45 km de Semarang et de Solo. A l'intérieur de Java (900 m d'altitude).
PREIS	$$$	PRIX	$$$
ZIMMER	7 Villen, 3 Bungalows, 7 Suiten, 1 Villa Bella Vista mit fünf Schlafzimmern.	CHAMBRE	7 villas, 3 bungalows, 7 suites. 1 villa Bella Vista avec cinq chambres à coucher.
KÜCHE	»Java Red« mit mediterran inspirierter Küche, »Java Green« mit leichten Gerichten.	RESTAURATION	Le « Java Red » et sa cuisine d'inspiration méditerranéenne et le « Java Green » et ses plats légers.
GESCHICHTE	Seit Dezember 2003 ein einzigartiges Resort.	HISTOIRE	Depuis décembre 2003, l'ancienne plantation de café hollandaise est devenu un hôtel unique en son genre.
X-FAKTOR	So schmeckt Java!	LE « PETIT PLUS »	Toutes les senteurs de Java !

Enchanted on Bali...

Four Seasons Resort Bali, Sayan

Enchanted on Bali

Ubud, the most famous artist's city on Bali, is beautiful without doubt– but also quite loud as well: with gamelan musicians on every corner, tinny pop music issuing from souvenir shop speakers and the roar of motorbikes in the streets. It is hard to believe that there's a whole different world only a few kilometres away. But in the mountains near Sayan one hears only bird calls and the murmur of the Ayung. Here the air is simultaneously so dense and clear that you can see every single leaf of the plants on the rice terraces, and the jungle glows in an endless array of almost supernatural green tones. The Four Seasons Bali at Sayan has been situated in the midst of this scenery for only a few years, but it is as if it had always belonged here. The modern and reduced design is not at all the kind that makes one shiver and where one prefers not to touch anything for fear of making fingerprints – old Balinese furniture, warm teakwood and light natural stone make the rooms into real living spaces. The spa offers traditional massages and flower petal baths; the restaurants feature both eastern and western menus as well as a breathtaking view of the river and the mountains shielding Ubud. Far, far away.

Book to pack: "A Tale fromBali" by Vicki Baum

Four Seasons Resort Bali
Gianyar, Ubud
Bali, Indonesien 80571
Tel. +62 (361) 97 75 77
Fax +62 (361) 97 75 88
Website: www.fourseasons.com
www.great-escapes-hotels.com

DIRECTIONS	35 km/22 miles north of Denpasar Airport, on the outskirts of the village of Sayan (transfer upon request).
RATES	$$$$
ROOMS	18 suites, 42 villas.
FOOD	Eastern and western cuisine as well as light, alternative dishes on the "Ayung Terrace", "The Riverside Café". Drinks in the "Jati Bar".
HISTORY	Opened in March 1998 to reflect the mystic landscape in the mountains near Sayan.
X-FACTOR	From nowhere else does Bali seem so beautiful.

Verzaubert auf Bali

Ubud, die berühmteste Künstlerstadt auf Bali, ist zweifellos schön – aber auch schön laut: mit Gamelanmusikern an den Ecken, blechernem Pop aus den Lautsprechern der Souvenirshops und knatternden Motorrädern auf den Straßen. Kann nur wenige Kilometer entfernt eine andere Welt beginnen? Sie kann. In den Bergen bei Sayan sind nur die Lockrufe der Vögel und das Rauschen des Ayung zu hören, hier ist die Luft so dicht und klar zugleich, dass jedes einzelne Blatt der Pflänzchen auf den Reisterrassen erkennbar wird, und der Dschungel leuchtet in unendlich vielen und fast übernatürlichen Grüntönen. Inmitten dieser Kulisse steht das Four Seasons Bali at Sayan – seit wenigen Jahren erst und doch so, als hätte es schon immer hierher gehört. Das moderne und reduzierte Design ist keines von der Sorte, bei der man leicht fröstelt und aus Sorge vor Fingerabdrücken lieber nichts anfasst – alte balinesische Möbel, warmes Teakholz und heller Naturstein machen die Räume zu wirklichen Wohnräumen. Im Spa werden traditionelle Massagen und Blütenbäder angeboten, in den Restaurants östliche wie westliche Menüs und ein zauberhafter Blick auf den Fluss und die Berge, hinter denen Ubud liegt. Weit, weit weg.

Buchtipp: »Liebe und Tod auf Bali« von Vicki Baum

Les deux visages de Bali

Ubud, la ville artistique la plus célèbre de Bali, est sans nul doute une belle ville – mais aussi bien bruyante avec les joueurs de gamelan aux coins des rues, la musique pop diffusée par les hauts-parleurs des magasins de souvenirs et les mobylettes qui pétaradent toute la journée. On a peine à croire qu'à quelques kilomètres d'ici, existe un autre univers. Dans les montagnes de Sayan, on n'entend en effet que le chant des oiseaux et le murmure de la rivière. Ici l'air est si limpide que l'on peut distinguer chaque feuille sur les rizières en terrasses. La jungle décline ses tons de vert presque à l'infini et sa luminosité semble presque surnaturelle. Dans ce décor est situé le Four Seasons Bali at Sayan – de construction récente même si on a l'impression qu'il a toujours été là. Sa décoration moderne et minimaliste n'est pas de celles qui donnent le frisson ni de celles où l'on préfère ne rien toucher par crainte de laisser des traces de doigts – ici les vieux meubles balinais, le bois de teck et les pierres naturelles de couleur claire rendent les pièces vraiment accueillantes. Le centre de remise en forme propose des massages traditionnels et des bains de pétales de fleurs, les restaurants des menus orientaux et occidentaux ainsi qu'une vue splendide sur la rivière et les montagnes.

Livre à emporter : « Sang et volupté à Bali » de Vicki Baum

ANREISE	35 km nördlich vom Flughafen Denpasar gelegen, am Rand des Dorfes Sayan (Transfer auf Wunsch).
PREIS	$$$$
ZIMMER	18 Suiten, 42 Villen.
KÜCHE	Östliche und westliche Küche sowie leichte alternative Gerichte im »Ayung Terrace«, »The Riverside Café«. Drinks in der »Jati Bar«.
GESCHICHTE	Im März 1998 und als Spiegelbild der mystischen Landschaft in den Bergen bei Sayan eröffnet.
X-FAKTOR	Nirgendwo sonst ist der Blick auf Bali so schön.

ACCÈS	Situé à 35 km au nord de l'aéroport de Denpasar, en bordure du village de Sayan (transfert sur demande).
PRIX	$$$$
CHAMBRES	18 suites, 42 villas.
RESTAURATION	Cuisine orientale et occidentale ainsi que repas légers au « Ayung Terrace » et au « The Riverside Café ». Drinks au « Jati Bar ».
HISTOIRE	Ouvert en mars 1998. Reflet du paysage mystique dans les montagnes de Sayan.
LE « PETIT PLUS »	La vue sur Bali n'est nulle part ailleurs aussi belle.

A Private Paradise...
Amankila, Manggis, Bali

Amankila, Manggis, Bali

A Private Paradise

Slowly descending stairs can have something very majestic and glamorous about it – just think of a curved stairwell in a castle garden, the sparkling show steps on a Hollywood stage or simply a gangway high above a runway. If you dream of experiencing this feeling but do not want to wait for your rich prince or famous president, you can try your luck in Amankila. Stairs are the symbol of this exclusive resort on Bali's east coast. Narrow steps, for instance, link all suites to the reception and restaurant area; small steps in a wall lead to canals full of lotus blossoms, and even a pool extends cascade-like down three large terraces to the sea. "Step by step" one also discovers the other details on this "peaceful hill", which is what the term Amankila means. There is the fairytale-like view of the coast and ocean, a play of light and shade in the elegant suites and a figure of a deity adorning a wall in the living room. Two of the island's most important temples – Lempuyang and Besakih – can be found within the hotel's immediate vicinity. After an excursion, a picnic in the hills above the Amankila awaits you, where you can get even closer to heaven.

Book to pack: "Lord Jim" by Joseph Conrad

Amankila	
P.O. Box 33	
Manggis 80871, Karangasem	
Bali, Indonesia	
Tel. +62 (363) 413 33	
Fax +62 (363) 415 55	
Email: amankila@amanresorts.com	
Website: www.amanresorts.com	
www.great-escapes-hotels.com	

DIRECTIONS	Situated on Bali's east coast, 1.5 hours or 15 minutes by helicopter from Denpasar Airport.
RATES	$$$$
ROOMS	34 individual suites, including 9 Deluxe Pool Suites and 1 Amankila Suite, which contains two pavilions.
FOOD	Indonesian, Asian and Western. Particularly lovely is tea time in the library with ginger tea and Balinese cake
HISTORY	Opened in 1992.
X-FACTOR	Privacy pure by fabulous pools.

Ein privates Paradies

Langsam eine Treppe hinunter zu steigen, kann etwas sehr
Majestätisches und Glamouröses haben – man denke nur
an eine geschwungene Freitreppe in einen Schlossgarten,
eine funkelnde Showtreppe oder einfach eine Gangway
hoch über dem Rollfeld. Wer von diesem Gefühl träumt,
aber nicht auf den reichen Prinzen oder berühmten Präsi-
denten warten will, kann im Amankila sein Glück versuchen. Das exklusive Resort an der Ostküste Balis hat Stufen
zu seinem Symbol erkoren. So sind zum Beispiel alle Suiten über schmale Treppen mit Rezeption und Restaurant-
bereich verbunden, kleine Mauertritte führen zu Kanälen
voller Lotusblüten, und sogar ein Pool zieht sich kaskaden-
artig über drei große Terrassen zum Meer hinab. Wie in
Schichten entdeckt man auch die weiteren Details auf dem
»friedlichen Hügel«, wie Amankila übersetzt heißt. Da ist
der märchenhafte Blick über die Küste und den Ozean, das
Spiel von Licht und Schatten in den eleganten Suiten und
die Götterfigur, die eine Wand im Wohnzimmer ziert. Ganz
in der Nähe des Hotels stehen übrigens zwei der wichtigsten
Tempel der Insel – Lempuyang und Besakih. Nach einem
Ausflug wartet ein Picknick in den Hügeln über dem Amankila, wo man dem Himmel noch ein Stück näher kommt.
Buchtipp: »Lord Jim« von Joseph Conrad

Un paradis pour soi

On peut descendre lentement un escalier avec majesté et glamour – il suffit de penser à l'escalier monumental d'un châ-
teau, à celui brillant de tous ses feux que nous montre le
show-biz ou tout simplement à la passerelle d'un avion.
Celui qui rêve d'éprouver cette sensation, tout en sachant
pertinemment qu'il ne sera jamais ni un prince fortuné ni
un président célèbre, peut tenter sa chance à Amankila. Le
très sélect hôtel sur la côte est de Bali a élevé l'escalier au
rang de symbole. Ainsi toutes les suites sont-elles reliées par
de petits escaliers à la réception et à la salle de restaurant,
des marches ménagées dans les murets conduisent aux bassins remplis de fleurs de lotus et l'une des piscines, étagée
sur trois terrasses, descend même en cascade jusqu'à la mer.
A Amankila, dont le nom signifie « la colline paisible », les
autres détails se découvrent successivement : la vue mer-
veilleuse sur la côte et l'océan, le jeu d'ombre et de lumière
dans les suites élégantes et les dieux qui ornent un mur de la
salle à manger. D'ailleurs deux des temples les plus importants de l'île se trouvent à proximité – Lempuyang et Besakih. Et l'une des excursions prévoit un pique-nique dans les
collines au-dessus d'Amankila, pour se rapprocher encore un
peu plus des cieux.
Livre à emporter : « Lord Jim » de Joseph Conrad

ANREISE	An der Ostküste von Bali gelegen, 1,5 Fahrtstunden oder 15 Helikopterminuten vom Flughafen Denpasar entfernt.
PREIS	$$$$
ZIMMER	34 freistehende Suiten, darunter 9 Deluxe Pool Suiten und 1 Amankila Suite, die zwei Pavillons umfasst.
KÜCHE	Indonesisch, asiatisch und westlich. Besonders schön: die Teestunde in der Bibliothek mit Ingwertee und bali- nesischen Kuchen.
GESCHICHTE	1992 eröffnet.
X-FAKTOR	Privatsphäre pur an herrlichen Pools.

ACCÈS	Situé sur la côte est de Bali, à 1 h ½ en voiture ou 15 min en hélicoptère de l'aéroport de Denpasar.
PRIX	$$$$
CHAMBRES	34 suites indépendantes, dont 9 suites de luxe avec piscine et 1 suite Amankila Suite, qui comprend 2 pavillons.
RESTAURATION	Cuisine asiatique et européenne. Thé au gingembre et gâteaux balinais dans la bibliothèque.
HISTOIRE	Ouvert en 1992.
LE « PETIT PLUS »	Intimité totale près des magnifiques piscines.

The Four Elements...
Como Shambhala Estate, Bali

The Four Elements

This is one of those "once in a lifetime" hotels – and one which you have to visit with all your heart. The five buildings that are hidden in the jungle behind Ubud between rice terraces and waterfalls at first seem a bit sinister and like a mirage, which threatens to dissolve the moment you extend your hand or breathe too heavily. But never fear, the wood from Bali, the stone from Sumba, the silk from Thailand and the porcelain from China are solid enough, turning the five buildings into deluxe jungle residences. And also into places where the four elements are always present: for example, as a cool breeze that drifts across the veranda, as a private campfire site, as untreated stone or a pool that seems to have no edge. If you travel to Como Shambhala Estate, you will rediscover nature and yourself – and not only during solitary yoga hours or meditation. The estate is surrounded by some of the most beautiful jogging paths on the island; three sacred springs are just a stroll away, and then in the spa "The Source" you can have a foot massage with Balinese oil. And who knows? Perhaps you will not leave it at just "once in a lifetime"...

Book to pack: "Bali: A Paradise Created" by Adrian Vickers

Como Shambhala Estate
P.O. Box 54, Ubud – 80571
Bali, Indonesia
Tel. +62 (361) 97 88 88
Fax +62 (361) 97 88 89
Email: info@cse.comoshambhala.bz
Website: www.cse.como.bz
www.great-escapes-hotels.com

DIRECTIONS	Situated 20 minutes north of Ubud, 1 hour from Denpasar Airport (40 km/25 miles, transfer upon request).
RATES	$$$$
ROOMS	22 individually furnished suites in 5 residences (one private butler per house).
FOOD	International, with an Indonesian touch. Served in the residences or in "Biji" restaurant.
HISTORY	Built in 1999 by Debbie and Bradley Gardner.
X-FACTOR	Superlative hotel and spa with just a hint of spiritual

Die vier Elemente

Es ist ein Hotel der Kategorie »Einmal im Leben« – und eines, auf das man sich mit ganzem Herzen einlassen muss. Die fünf Häuser, die im Dschungel hinter Ubud verborgen stehen, zwischen Reisterrassen und Wasserfällen, wirken auf den ersten Blick ein wenig unheimlich und wie eine Fata Morgana, die sich aufzulösen droht, sobald man die Hand nach ihr ausstreckt oder auch nur zu heftig ausatmet. Doch keine Sorge, das Holz aus Bali, der Stein aus Sumba, die Seide aus Thailand und das Porzellan aus China halten der Berührung durchaus stand und machen die fünf Gebäude zu Dschungelresidenzen de luxe. Und zu Orten, an denen die vier Elemente allgegenwärtig sind; als kühle Brise über der Veranda zum Beispiel, als private Feuerstelle, unbearbeiteter Stein oder scheinbar randloser Pool. Wer nach Como Shambhala Estate kommt, soll die Natur und sich selbst wiederfinden – und das nicht nur bei einsamen Yogastunden oder Meditationen. Ringsum das Anwesen verlaufen einige der schönsten Joggingstrecken der Insel, drei heilige Quellen liegen nur eine Wanderung entfernt, und im Spa »The Source« werden die Füße anschließend mit balinesischen Ölen massiert. Und wer weiß? Vielleicht belässt man es ja dann doch nicht bei »Einmal im Leben«...

Buchtipp: »Bali. Ein Paradies wird erfunden«
von Adrian Vickers

Les quatre éléments

Cet hôtel fait partie de ceux dont on sait qu'on n'y séjournera qu'une fois dans sa vie et dont il faut savourer pleinement les journées. Les cinq bâtiments, cachés dans la jungle derrière la ville d'Ubud, entre les rizières et les cascades, suscitent au premier abord une impression bizarre, on dirait un mirage que l'on craint de voir s'évanouir si l'on a le malheur de tendre la main vers lui ou de respirer un peu trop fort. Mais n'ayez crainte le bois de Bali, la pierre de Sumba, la soie de Thaïlande et la porcelaine de Chine sont bien réels, transformant les cinq constructions en résidences de luxe. Et en lieux où les quatre éléments sont omniprésents : que ce soit sous la forme d'une légère brise soufflant sur la véranda, d'un feu de camp, de la pierre laissée à l'état brut ou de la piscine semblant dépourvue de bord. Celui qui vient à Como Shambhala Estate, doit redécouvrir la nature et se redécouvrir lui-même. Il y parviendra pendant les cours de yoga et de méditation, mais aussi par le biais du footing car quelques-unes des plus belles pistes de l'île entourent le complexe hôtelier. Trois sources sacrées se trouvent à quelques heures de marche seulement et dans le centre de remise en forme « The Source », les pieds bénéficieront d'un délicieux massage avec des huiles balinaises. Et qui sait ? peut-être reviendrons-nous...

Livre à emporter : « Bali et les petites îles de la Sonde »
de Liz Capaldi, Joshua Eliot.

ANREISE	20 Fahrtminuten nördlich von Ubud gelegen, 1 Fahrtstunde vom Flughafen Denpasar entfernt (40 km, Transfer auf Wunsch).
PREIS	$$$$
ZIMMER	22 individuell ausgestattete Suiten in 5 Residenzen (ein Privatbutler pro Haus).
KÜCHE	International, mit indonesischen Akzenten. Serviert in den Residenzen oder im Restaurant »Biji«.
GESCHICHTE	Von Debbie und Bradley Gardner 1999 gebaut.
X-FAKTOR	Hotel und Spa der Superlative; spirituell angehaucht.

ACCÈS	Situé à 20 min en voiture au nord d'Ubud, à 1 h en voiture de l'aéroport de Denpasar (40 km, transfert sur demande).
PRIX	$$$$
CHAMBRES	22 suites aménagées individuellement dans 5 résidences (un majordome par maison).
RESTAURATION	Internationale, teintée d'influences indonésiennes. Plats servis dans les résidences ou au restaurant « Biji ».
HISTOIRE	Construit en 1999 par Debbie et Bradley Gardner.
LE « PETIT PLUS »	Hôtel et centre de remise en forme pour lesquels on ne peut employer que des superlatifs.

A Room with a View...
Taman Selini, Bali

Taman Selini, Bali

A Room with a View

They can only be seen early in the morning and only by those who watch the ocean with great patience: the dolphins shoot up like tense, slightly chubby arches and spray water as they dive back in. Their favourite spots are off of Bali's northwest coast; there, where fewer ships sail than in the south, where the dark beaches are more secluded and the face of the island creases into gentle wrinkles. The volcanic mountain chain also forms a backdrop for the bungalows of Taman Belini in Pemuteran. The fishing village is not only an address for the small resort; it is also a home to the locals. The buildings were primarily built by local craftsmen using Balinese materials. Many village residents took part in English classes and cooking courses and now tend to the guests of Taman Selini, and inviting foreign visitors to family celebrations or religious ceremonies is nothing unusual. The bungalows attain an unusual balance: You feel both like a guest and at home. You enjoy tea on the terrace with a view of the ocean. You take walks through the garden and touch the enchanting flowers of the bougainvilleas, frangipanis and jacarandas, just to check whether they are real or actually coloured plastic. And voluntarily get up early every morning – just because of the dolphins.

Book to pack: "The Islands" by Albert Alberts

Taman Selini

Beach Bungalows
Desa Pemuteran, Gerogkak,
Singaraja, Bali, Indonesia
Tel. +62 (362) 947 46
Fax +62 (362) 947 46
Email: reservation@tamanselini.com
Website: www.tamanselini.com
www.great-escapes-hotels.com

DIRECTIONS	Situated in Pemuteran on the northwest coast of Bali, 10 km / 6 miles west of Singaraja (4 hours to the airport, the transport is organized).
RATES	$
ROOMS	11 bungalows.
FOOD	Simple Balinese dishes. Occasional Greek specialties as well.
HISTORY	Built by a Balinese-Greek couple.
X-FACTOR	Far away but still feels like home.

Zimmer mit Aussicht

Sie zeigen sich nur früh am Morgen und nur denen, die mit viel Geduld aufs Meer hinausschauen: die Delfine, die wie gespannte, ein wenig dickliche Bogen aus dem Wasser schnellen und spritzend wieder untertauchen. Ihre Lieblingsplätze liegen vor der Nordwestküste Balis, dort, wo weniger Schiffe fahren als im Süden, die dunklen Strände einsamer sind und das Gesicht der Insel zarte Falten zeigt. Die vulkanische Bergkette bildet auch die Kulisse für die Bungalows von Taman Belini in Pemuteran. Das Fischerdorf ist für die kleine Anlage nicht nur eine Adresse – es ist eine Heimat. So wurden die Häuser hauptsächlich aus balinesischen Materialien und von hiesigen Handwerkern erbaut, viele Dorfbewohner nahmen an Englisch- und Kochkursen teil und kümmern sich jetzt um die Gäste von Taman Selini. Und dass die gerade noch fremden Besucher zu Familienfesten oder religiösen Zeremonien eingeladen werden, ist keine Seltenheit. Die Bungalows schaffen einen seltenen Spagat: Man fühlt sich in ihnen zu Gast und zu Hause zugleich. Genießt den Tee auf der Terrasse mit Blick aufs Meer, testet beim Spaziergang durch den Garten, ob die zauberhaften Blüten der Bougainvilleen, Frangipanis und Jakarandas wirklich echt oder nicht doch aus farbigem Plastik sind. Und steht jeden Morgen freiwillig früh auf – einzig um der Delfine willen.

Buchtipp: »Die Inseln« von Albert Alberts

Une chambre avec vue

Les dauphins ne se montrent qu'à ceux qui se lèvent tôt et ont de la patience. Ils surgissent alors des flots comme des arcs tendus, un peu rondelets, pour y replonger dans un grand jet d'écume. Leurs endroits préférés sont situés devant la côte nord-ouest de Bali : là où la circulation est moins dense que dans le Sud, là où les plages sombres sont plus isolées et où le visage de l'île montre des rides délicates. La chaîne de massifs volcaniques sert aussi de décor aux bungalows de Taman Selini à Pemuteran.

Le village de pêcheurs n'est pas seulement une adresse mais une patrie, les maisons ont essentiellement été construites à l'aide de matériaux balinais et par des artisans de la région ; de nombreux villageois ont pris des cours d'anglais et des cours de cuisine et s'occupent maintenant des hôtes de Taman Selini – il n'est pas rare que les visiteurs encore inconnus soient invités à participer aux fêtes de famille et aux cérémonies religieuses.

Les bungalows réussissent à concilier deux aspects paradoxaux puisque l'on s'y sent chez soi et aussi en visite chez des amis. On se détend en buvant le thé sur la terrasse avec vue sur la mer, on hume en se promenant dans le jardin les fleurs éblouissantes des bougainvillées, des frangipaniers et des jacarandas – les unes ont une odeur, les autres pas. Et on se lève de bonne heure le matin uniquement pour pouvoir observer les dauphins.

Livre à emporter : «The Islands» de Albert Alberts

ANREISE	In Pemuteran an der Nordwestküste Balis gelegen, 10 km westlich von Singaraja (4 Fahrtstunden zum Flughafen, Transfer wird organisiert).
PREIS	$
ZIMMER	11 Bungalows.
KÜCHE	Einfache balinesische Gerichte. Gelegentlich auch griechische Spezialitäten.
GESCHICHTE	Von einem balinesisch-griechischen Ehepaar erbaut.
X-FAKTOR	Weit weg und trotzdem zu Hause sein.

ACCÈS	Situé à Pemuteran sur la côte nord-ouest de Bali, à 10 km à l'ouest de Singaraja (4 h de voiture jusqu'à l'aéroport, transfert organisé).
PRIX	$
CHAMBRES	11 bungalows.
RESTAURATION	Cuisine balinaise simple. A l'occasion spécialités grecques.
HISTOIRE	Construit par un couple gréco-balinais.
LE «PETIT PLUS»	Se sentir chez soi au bout du monde.

A Dream Becomes Reality...

The Oberoi, Bali

The Oberoi, Bali

In the Garden of Eden

Many think of southern Bali as a stomping ground for loud and hyperactive tourists – but the truth is that here too there are secluded glimpses of paradise, with golden beaches, magical tropical gardens and hotels that are a dream. The Oberoi Bali is just a few kilometres from the airport, but it might be another world entirely. The 60 straw-roofed lanais and 15 villas make up a small, snug village right on Seminyak Beach; eight of these luxurious accommodations even have their own private pool. The rooms are appointed in teak, with Balinese art, and from the bathroom you look out into your own garden. Even the spa keeps you on intimate terms with nature: the open-air massage pavilions are out in the greenery, where the warm air and the fragrance of exotic plants perfectly complement the treatment and veritably transform the experience into an all-in work of art. True to the overall style, the hotel restaurant bears what must surely be the loveliest name on the whole island: at the Frangipani Café you can take a light lunch and excellent seafood. A vacation at the Oberoi Bali seems to pass at a more leisurely pace than anywhere else – and that is as it should be. After all, you want the days to be free of the pressures of the appointments diary, and to leave you the time and space to converse with the statue of a deity, or count the lotus blossoms in the pond.

Book to pack: "The Mysterious Island" by Jules Verne

The Oberoi Bali
P. O. Box 3351
Denpasar 80033
Bali
Indonesia
Tel. (62) 361 73 03 61
Fax (62) 361 73 00 791
E-mail: Gm.Tobi@oberoihotels.com
Website: www.oberoihotels.com
www.great-escapes-hotels.com

DIRECTIONS	9 km / 5 miles north of Bali's international airport (transfer is organised on request).
RATES	$$$
ROOMS	60 lanais and 15 villas.
FOOD	3 restaurants serving Indonesian and international cuisine, 1 bar. Extras: several times a week there are Balinese evenings featuring Balinese dancing.
HISTORY	Conceived in the spirit of a traditional village, but with every modern luxury.
X-FACTOR	All the romantic tranquillity you could desire.

Im Garten Eden

Den Süden Balis kennen viele nur als lauten und lebhaften Tummelplatz der Touristen – doch weit gefehlt: Auch hier gibt es versteckte Paradiese mit goldfarbenen Stränden, verwunschenen Tropengärten und traumhaften Hotels. The Oberoi Bali liegt nur wenige Kilometer vom Flughafen entfernt, aber wie in einer anderen Welt. 60 strohgedeckte Lanais und 15 Villen bilden ein kleines, in die Umgebung wunderbar integriertes Dorf direkt am Seminyak-Strand; acht der Luxusunterkünfte besitzen sogar einen privaten Pool. Die Zimmer sind mit Teakholz und balinesischer Kunst ausgestattet, und vom Bad aus blickt man direkt in den eigenen Garten. Auf Tuchfühlung mit der Natur gehen die Gäste übrigens selbst im Spa: Die Open-air-Massagepavillons stehen direkt im Grünen, so dass die warme Luft und der Duft exotischer Pflanzen die Behandlungen perfekt ergänzen und fast zu einem Gesamtkunstwerk machen. Ganz stilgetreu besitzt das Hotel auch das Restaurant mit dem vielleicht hübschesten Namen der Insel: Im Frangipani Café werden leichter Lunch und ausgezeichnetes Seafood serviert. Urlaubstage im Oberoi Bali scheinen langsamer zu vergehen als anderswo – und das ist auch gut so: Schließlich sollen die Tage terminkalenderlos verstreichen und genug Raum für ein Zwiegespräch mit der Götterstatue gegenüber lassen oder für das Zählen der Lotusblüten im Teich.

Buchtipp: »Die geheimnisvolle Insel« von Jules Verne

Dans le jardin d'Eden

Nombreux sont ceux qui ne connaissent du sud de Bali que les endroits agités et bruyants réservés aux touristes, mais il existe ici aussi des paradis cachés aux plages dorées, avec des jardins tropicaux enchanteurs et des hôtels de rêve. The Oberoi Bali n'est situé qu'à quelques kilomètres de l'aéroport et pourtant on se croirait transporté dans un autre univers. 60 lanais aux toits recouverts de chaume et 15 villas forment un petit village avec accès direct à la plage de Seminyak. Huit des logements de luxe possèdent même une piscine privée. Les chambres sont meublées en bois de teak et décorées avec des œuvres d'art balinaises. De la salle de bains, on a une vue magnifique sur les jardins. Les clients restent d'ailleurs en contact avec la nature même dans le centre de remise en forme : les pavillons de massage sont ouverts de tous les côtés, au milieu d'une végétation luxuriante. Impossible de ne pas se détendre avec cette légère brise qui vous caresse la peau et le parfum des plantes exotiques qui embaume l'air. L'hôtel possède aussi le restaurant qui a peut-être le plus joli nom de toute l'île, le café Frangipani, où l'on vous servira des repas légers et des plats incomparables à base de poissons. Ici, les vacances semblent s'écouler à un rythme plus serein qu'ailleurs – et c'est bien ici, car ces jours passés sans rendez-vous vous laisseront le temps de converser avec les statues des dieux ou de compter les fleurs de lotus dans l'étang.

Livre à emporter : « L'Ile mystérieuse » de Jules Verne

ANREISE	9 km nördlich vom Internationalen Flughafen Balis gelegen (Transfer wird auf Wunsch organisiert).
PREIS	$$$
ZIMMER	60 Lanais und 15 Villen.
KÜCHE	3 Restaurants mit indonesischer und internationaler Küche, 1 Bar. Extras: Mehrmals wöchentlich balinesische Abende mit Tanzvorführungen.
GESCHICHTE	Einem traditionellen Dorf nachempfunden, aber mit allem Luxus der Gegenwart.
X-FAKTOR	Viel Ruhe und Romantik.

ACCÈS	Situé à 9 kilomètres au nord de l'aéroport international de Bali (le transfert est organisé sur demande).
PRIX	$$$
CHAMBRES	60 lanais et 15 villas.
RESTAURATION	3 restaurants proposant une cuisine indonésienne et internationale, 1 bar. Extras : soirées balinaises avec danses plusieurs fois par semaine.
HISTOIRE	Reconstitution d'un village traditionnel avec le luxe en plus.
LE « PETIT PLUS »	Beaucoup de calme et de romantisme.

Between Sky and Sea...

Amanpulo, Pamalican Island

Amanpulo, Pamalican Island

Between Sky and Sea

Don't let yourself be misled by the word Amanpulo which means "peaceful island". A visit to this island will definitely not be peaceful in the boring sense of the word. Because a fantastic reef encircles Amanpulo, making the small private island 300 kilometres south of Manila one of the best things that could happen to water sports fans. Underwater, divers feel like they are in a gigantic 3-D picture filled with maritime motifs; skippers see how many beaches they can visit while island hopping for the day and counting the whales, dolphins or sea cows between the waves, and romantics sail through the sunset right into the moonlight. One could almost worry that the dry land has nothing to offer in contrast to the sea – but this is far from the case. The 40 *casitas* of Amanpulo are small dream houses, built in a traditional Philippine way and furnished with favourite spots like hammocks and observation terraces. If you live at the ocean, a private woodland path leads to the beach; if you go up in the hills, you enjoy even more peace, a view that is at most slightly obstructed by the greenery of the neighbouring islands and with a bit of luck a *casita* from whose veranda you can watch both sunrise and sunset. Whichever house you reside in, almost half of the living space is taken up by a splendid marble bath – even where it is dry, everything here has to do with water.

Book to pack: "Infanta" by Bodo Kirchoff

Amanpulo

Pamalican Island, Philippines
Tel. + 63 (2) 759 40 40
Fax + 63 (2) 759 40 44
Email: amanpulo@amanresorts.com
Website: www.amanresorts.com
www.great-escapes-hotels.com

DIRECTIONS	The private island of Pamalican is situated 300 km / 186 miles south of Manila; the transfer via aircraft is organized (US$ 300 per person).
RATES	$$$$
ROOMS	4 treetop casitas, 7 hillside casitas, 29 beach casitas, 2 villas.
FOOD	Fantastic seafood, as well as Asian dishes and barbecue on the beach.
HISTORY	Opened in 1993.
X-FACTOR	Beach, sun, sailboats – paradise complete.

Zwischen Himmel und Meer

Amanpulo heißt übersetzt »friedliche Insel« – doch lassen Sie sich nicht täuschen: friedlich im Sinne von langweilig wird es hier ganz bestimmt nicht. Denn rund um Amanpulo zieht sich ein fantastisches Riff und macht die kleine Privatinsel 300 Kilometer südlich von Manila zum Besten, was Wassersportlern passieren kann. Taucher fühlen sich in der Unterwasserwelt wie in einem gigantischen 3-D-Bild voller maritimer Motive, Skipper testen aus, wie viele Strände sie innerhalb eines Island-Hopping-Days anlaufen können und zählen zwischen den Wellen Wale, Delfine oder Seekühe, und Romantiker segeln durch den Sonnenuntergang geradewegs ins Mondlicht. Man hat fast ein wenig Sorge, das Festland könne den Geheimnissen des Meeres nichts entgegensetzen – doch dies ist unbegründet. Die 40 *Casitas* von Amanpulo sind kleine Traumhäuser; gebaut nach traditioneller philippinischer Art und mit Lieblingsplätzen wie Hängematten oder Aussichtsterrassen ausgestattet. Wer am Ozean wohnt, erreicht den Strand über einen privaten Buschpfad; wer hinauf in die Hügel zieht, genießt noch mehr Ruhe, höchstens von etwas Grün verstellte Sicht auf die Nachbarinseln und mit etwas Glück eine *Casita*, von deren Veranda aus sowohl Sonnenaufgang als auch Sonnenuntergang zu sehen sind. Und egal, für welches Haus man sich entscheidet: Beinahe die Hälfte der Wohnfläche nimmt ein prächtiges Marmorbad ein – selbst auf dem Trockenen dreht sich hier eben alles ums Wasser.

Buchtipp: »Infanta« von Bodo Kirchoff

Entre le ciel et la mer

Amanpulo signifie « l'île paisible », mais, soyez sans inquiétude, vous ne vous y ennuierez certainement pas. En effet, Amanpulo est entourée d'une sublime barrière de corail qui fait de la petite île privée située à 300 kilomètres au sud de Manille un véritable paradis pour les amateurs de sports aquatiques. Les plongeurs ont l'impression de se trouver dans un film présentant les merveilles sous-marines, les skippers cherchent combien de plages ils peuvent accoster en un Island-Hopping-Day et comptent les baleines, les dauphins et les lamantins qui surgissent au creux des vagues ; quant aux romantiques, il naviguent pendant que le soleil se couche pour jouir ensuite du clair de lune.
On craindrait presque que l'île ne puisse être à la hauteur de la mer qui l'entoure et de ses mystères – mais ce n'est pas le cas. Les 40 *casitas* d'Amanpulo ne sont pas des demeures de rêve, mais des maisons philippines traditionnelles équipées de hamacs ou de terrasses d'où l'on peut contempler le paysage par exemple. Celui qui habite près de l'océan, accède à la plage par un sentier privé ; celui qui s'installe sur les collines, jouit encore plus du calme, bénéficie d'une vue sur les îles voisines que lui cache tout au plus la végétation et, s'il a de la chance, il peut admirer le lever et le coucher de soleil de sa véranda. Mais qu'importe l'endroit choisi : une superbe salle de bains en marbre occupe près de la moitié de l'habitation – même sur la terre ferme, tout tourne autour de l'eau.

Livre à emporter : « Infanta » de Bodo Kirchhoff

ANREISE	Die Privatinsel Pamalican liegt 300 km südlich von Manila, der Transfer per Flugzeug wird organisiert (300 $ pro Person).
PREIS	$$$$
ZIMMER	4 Treetop Casitas, 7 Hillside Casitas, 29 Beach Casitas, 2 Villen.
KÜCHE	Fantastische Meeresfrüchte, außerdem asiatische Gerichte und Barbecue am Strand.
GESCHICHTE	1993 eröffnet.
X-FAKTOR	Strand, Sonne, Segelboote – fertig ist das Paradies.

ACCÈS	L'île privée de Pamalican est située à 300 km au sud de Manille, le transfert par avion est organisé (300 $ par personne).
PRIX	$$$$
CHAMBRES	4 Treetop Casitas, 7 Hillside Casitas, 29 Beach Casitas, 2 villas.
RESTAURATION	Fruits de mer fantastiques, cuisine asiatique et barbecue sur la plage.
HISTOIRE	Ouvert en 1993.
LE « PETIT PLUS »	Le soleil, la plage et les voiliers, qui dit mieux ?

A Living Room by the Sea...

The Barceló Pearl Farm Island Resort, Samal Island

The Barceló Pearl Farm Island Resort, Samal Island

A Living Room by the Sea

If you travel to the tropics and step from a propeller-driven plane onto a runway the size of a towel or step outside after having been in a thoroughly air-conditioned room, the blast of heat is often like a concrete wall. For seconds your air supply seems to have been shut off and if you close your eyes you feel like you are in a sauna where some eager punter has just poured more water onto the stones. Unless, that is, the trip happens to takes you to Samal Island. Here in the Gulf of Davao you immerse yourself in the warmth like in a large tub filled with gentle water and you inhale the scent of sea salt, exotic fruits and plants so green that the chlorophyll almost colours the air. The Barceló Pearl Farm Beach Resort is situated in this world of wonders and its most beautiful rooms can be found in the Samal House directly by the ocean. The houses were built based on the traditional stilt houses of the Samal seafarers. One glimpse of the colourful swarms of fish swimming through the crystal-clear water is enough to easily convince you that you will have no need for the television in the back room. On Samal Island, modern technology is just a concession to modern times; the rooms with their slight ethnic touch are intended primarily to reflect the beauty of their surroundings.

Homes and nature are mostly linked by wooden footbridges and even by rope ladders – a more beautiful way of getting from the living room to the beach does not exist!

Book to pack: "Playing with Water" by James Hamilton-Paterson

The Barceló Pearl Farm Island Resort	
Kaputian, Island Garden City of Samal	
Davao del Norte, Philippines	
Tel. +632 433 75 32	
Email: deals@kolobialtravel.com	
Website: www.barcelopearl.com	
www.great-escapes-hotels.com	

DIRECTIONS	Samal Island is situated south of Manila at the Gulf of Davao, 1.5 hours by air and then 45 minutes by boat.
RATES	$$
ROOMS	19 Samal Houses with a total of 22 rooms, 6 Samal Suites, 41 rooms in the Balay, Mandaya and Hilltop Houses, 7 Malipano Villas.
FOOD	Typical Filipino, the seafood is particularly good.
HISTORY	Opened in December 1992. The spa "Ylang-Ylang Soothing Lounge" was added recently.
X-FACTOR	Experience the unspoilt Philippines and modern luxury.

Ein Wohnzimmer am Wasser

Wenn man in die Tropen reist und auf einem handtuch-
großen Rollfeld aus der Propellermaschine steigt oder aus
einem gut klimatisierten Hotelzimmer ins Freie tritt, trifft
einen die Hitze oft wie eine Betonwand. Für Sekunden
scheint die Luft zum Atmen abgedreht, und wer die Augen
schließt, fühlt sich in eine Sauna versetzt, in der ein besonders Schwitzbedürftiger eben erst einen Aufguss über die
Steine geschüttet hat. Es sei denn, die Reise führt nach
Samal Island. Hier, im Golf von Davao, versinkt man in der
Wärme wie in einer großen, mit weichem Wasser gefüllten
Wanne und atmet den Duft nach Meersalz, exotischen
Früchten und Pflanzen, die so sattgrün sind, dass das Chlo-
rophyll beinahe die Luft färbt. In dieser Wunderwelt steht
das Barceló Pearl Farm Beach Resort, dessen schönste
Unterkünfte, die Samal Houses, direkt am Ozean stehen.
Sie wurden den traditionellen Stelzenhäusern des Seefahrer-
stammes der Samal nachempfunden – wer den Blick auf
die bunten Fischschwärme, die durchs kristallklare Wasser
ziehen, einmal erlebt hat, könnte ohne weiteres auf den
Fernseher im rückwärtigen Zimmer verzichten. Moderne
Technik ist auf Samal Island ohnehin nur ein Zugeständnis
an moderne Zeiten, die Räume mit leichtem Ethno-Touch
sollen in erster Linie die Schönheit ihrer Umgebung wider-
spiegeln. Verbunden sind Häuser und Natur übrigens meist
über hölzerne Stege und sogar über Strickleitern – eine
schönere Art, vom Wohnzimmer zum Strand zu gelangen,
gibt es nicht!
Buchtipp: »Wasserspiele« von James Hamilton-Paterson

Un salon dans l'eau

Sous les Tropiques, le voyageur qui descend de l'avion à
hélices et se retrouve sur une piste grande comme un mou-
choir de poche ou qui sort de son hôtel climatisé se heurte
à la chaleur comme à un mur en béton. Pendant quelques
secondes, il a l'impression qu'il n'a plus d'air pour respirer,
et en fermant les yeux il lui semble se trouver dans un bain
de vapeur dont la température aurait été forcée par un visiteur trop bien intentionné. Celui qui se rend à Samal Island
ne connaît pas ces vicissitudes. Ici, dans le golfe de Davao,
la chaleur vous enveloppe comme l'eau tiède et douce dans
une grande baignoire, l'air marin est chargé de senteurs de
fruits exotiques et de plantes si vertes que la chlorophylle
semble colorer l'atmosphère.

Le Barceló Pearl Farm Resort est situé dans ce monde merveilleux, dont les plus belles résidences, les Samal Houses,
sont placées au bord de l'océan. Elles imitent les traditionnelles maisons sur pilotis des Samal, un peuple de naviga-
teurs. Celui qui a vu les bancs de poissons multicolores se
déplacer dans l'eau limpide peut renoncer sans regret au
téléviseur dont sa maison est équipée.

De toute façon, à Samal Island, la technologie moderne
n'est qu'une concession à l'époque actuelle, les pièces qui
montrent une légère touche ethno doivent avant tout refléter
la beauté de leur environnement. Du reste, les maisons et
la nature sont reliées le plus souvent par des passerelles en
bois et même en corde – il n'y a pas de plus belle manière
de passer du salon à la plage.
Livre à emporter : « Le dieu volé et autres nouvelles »
de José Francisco Sionil

ANREISE	Samal Island liegt im Golf von Davao, 1,5 Flugstunden und weitere 45 Bootsminuten südlich von Manila.
PREIS	$$
ZIMMER	19 Samal Houses mit insgesamt 22 Zimmern, 6 Samal-Suiten, 41 Zimmer in den Balay, Mandaya und Hilltop Houses, 7 Malipano-Villen.
KÜCHE	Typisch philippinisch, besonders gut ist das Seafood.
GESCHICHTE	Im Dezember 1992 eröffnet. Seit kurzem auch mit dem Spa »Ylang-Ylang Soothing Lounge«.
X-FAKTOR	Die ursprünglichen Philippinen und modernen Luxus erleben.

ACCÈS	Samal Island est située dans le golfe de Davao, à 1 h ½ de vol et 45 min de bateau du sud de Manille.
PRIX	$$
CHAMBRES	19 Samal Houses abritant 22 chambres, 6 suites Samal, 41 chambres dans les Balay, Mandaya et Hill-top Houses, 7 villas Malipano.
RESTAURATION	Cuisine traditionnelle philippine, les plats de poisson.
HISTOIRE	Ouvert en décembre 1992. Il abrite depuis peu de temps un centre de remise en forme « Ylang-Ylang Soothing Lounge ».
LE « PETIT PLUS »	Les Philippines traditionnelles avec le luxe moderne.

In the Shade of the Palms...
Whale Island Resort, Ile de la Baleine

Whale Island Resort, Ile de la Baleine

In the Shade of the Palms

The Frenchman Michel Galey and his wife had just com-
pleted a taxing trekking tour through the highlands of Vietnam and were in need of a little peace and relaxation on
level ground. They chartered a boat at Van Phong Bay, sailed
through the bay northeast of Nha Trang and discovered their
own personal paradise: Whale Island, a small private island
with the best of what the tropics have to offer. Bays with
white sandy beaches, palm trees whose leaves rustle in the
wind and swimming in crystal-clear waters accompanied by
swarms of tiny shining fish. As of 1997 visitors have been
able to share this picture-book island with the couple: Whale
Island has become an enchanting refuge in the truest sense
of the word. The route through the coastal landscape would
challenge even the most adept boy scout, which is why every
new arrival is picked up in Nha Trang and brought to the
pier in Dam Mon, where the boats depart for the brief final
leg of the journey. On Whale Island you live in simple
bungalows, whose apparent lack of comfort is more than
made up for by an unforgettable view of the beach, the
warm-heartedness of the hosts and the seafood cuisine –
a vacation at your best friend's could not be better. Between
mid-January and mid-October, divers in particular are in
their watery element. The maritime life around the bay's
reef is a dazzling display of colour. Jacques Cousteau is
said to have discovered his love of diving here.

**Book to pack: "The Girl in the Picture: The Story of Kim Phuc"
by Denise Chong**

Whale Island Resort
Ile de la Baleine, Vietnam
Tel. +84 (58) 84 05 01
Fax +84 (58) 84 05 01
Website: www.iledelabaleine.com
www.great-escapes-hotels.com

DIRECTIONS	Situated about 140 km/87 miles northeast of Nha Trang (the two-and-a-half hour transfer from the airport).
RATES	$
ROOMS	20 bungalows directly on the beach, 5 budget rooms.
FOOD	Daily changing Vietnamese specialities; primarily seafood.
HISTORY	Opened in 1997 as a prime example of peaceful tourism.
X-FACTOR	Pure nature in an entirely private paradise.

Im Schatten der Palmen

Der Franzose Michel Galey und seine Frau hatten eine anstrengende Trekkingtour durchs Hochland Vietnams hinter sich und wollten nur noch Ruhe und Erholung auf möglichst ebener Fläche. An der Van Phong Bay charterten sie ein Boot, segelten durch die Bucht nordöstlich von Nha Trang – und entdeckten ihr ganz persönliches Paradies: Whale Island, eine kleine Privatinsel mit dem Besten, was die Tropen zu bieten haben. Buchten mit weißen Sandstränden, Palmen, deren Blätter im Wind rascheln, und kristallklares Wasser, in dem man beim Schwimmen von Schwärmen winziger, leuchtend bunter Fische begleitet wird. Seit 1997 können Besucher diese Bilderbuchinsel mit den beiden teilen: Whale Island ist ein zauberhaftes Refugium geworden – und das im wahrsten Sinne des Wortes. Die Anfahrt durch die Küstenlandschaft überfordert selbst versierte Pfadfinder, deshalb wird jeder Neuankömmling in Nha Trang abgeholt und zum Pier von Dam Mon gebracht, wo die Boote für die kurze Passage ablegen. Auf Whale Island wohnt man in schlichten Bungalows, deren vermeintlich fehlender Komfort durch einen unvergesslichen Blick über den Strand, die Herzlichkeit der Gastgeber und die Seafood-Küche mehr als wettgemacht wird – Ferien bei den besten Freunden könnten nicht besser gelingen. Zwischen Mitte Januar und Mitte Oktober sind hier vor allem Taucher im nassen Element. Das maritime Leben rund um die Riffe der Bucht ist ein Feuerwerk der Farben, schon Jacques Cousteau soll hier seine Leidenschaft fürs Tauchen entdeckt haben.

Buchtipp: »Das Mädchen hinter dem Foto. Die Geschichte der Kim Phuc« von Denise Chong

A l'ombre des palmiers

Le Français Michel Galey et sa femme ayant terminé leur épuisant trekking à travers les hauts plateaux du Viêt-nam, ne souhaitaient plus qu'une chose, trouver calme et détente, dans un endroit plat si possible. Ils louèrent un bateau sur la baie Van Phong, naviguèrent au nord-est de Nha Trang et découvrirent leur paradis : l'Ile de la Baleine, une petite île privée, qui offraient tous les charmes des tropiques. Criques aux plages de sable blanc, cocotiers crissant sous le vent et des eaux limpides dans lesquelles des multitudes de poissons minuscules et multicolores accompagnent le nageur. Depuis 1997, les deux Français partagent leur île de carte postale avec les visiteurs. L'Ile de la Baleine est devenue un véritable refuge car il faut dire que l'accès par la côte découragerait même des randonneurs chevronnés. Les nouveaux venus sont attendus à Nha Trang et conduits jusqu'à la jetée de Dam Mon où sont ancrés les bateaux qui effectuent la traversée. A l'Ile de la Baleine, le client habite dans de simples bungalows dont l'apparente rusticité est compensée au centuple par une vue inoubliable sur la plage, l'accueil chaleureux des hôtes et la cuisine de fruits de mer. Des vacances chez des amis ne se passeraient pas dans de meilleures conditions. Entre la mi-janvier et la mi-octobre, les plongeurs peuvent s'en donner à cœur joie. Les fonds marins autour des récifs offrent un feu d'artifice de couleurs, et c'est ici que Jacques Cousteau aurait découvert sa passion pour la plongée sous-marine.

Livre à emporter : « La fille de la photo » de Denise Chong

ANREISE	Rund 140 km nordöstlich von Nha Trang gelegen (zweieinhalbstündiger Transfer ab dem Flughafen).
PREIS	$
ZIMMER	20 Bungalows direkt am Strand, 5 Economy Rooms.
KÜCHE	Täglich wechselnde vietnamesische Spezialitäten, vor allem Seafood.
GESCHICHTE	1997 als Musterbeispiel für sanften Tourismus eröffnet.
X-FAKTOR	Natur pur im ganz privaten Paradies.

ACCÈS	Situé à 140 km environ au nord-est de Nha Trang (le transfert de deux heures et demie depuis l'aéroport).
PRIX	$
CHAMBRES	20 bungalows donnant directement sur la plage, 5 Economic Rooms.
RESTAURATION	Tous les jours différentes spécialités vietnamiennes, en particulier fruits de mer.
HISTOIRE	Construit en 1997, l'hôtel est un exemple de tourisme modéré.
LE « PETIT PLUS »	Un petit paradis privé où la nature est reine.

Naturally Beautiful...
Evason Ana Mandara Resort, Nha Trang

Evason Ana Mandara Resort, Nha Trang

Naturally Beautiful

On the beach at Nha Trang, Vietnam shows its polished side. The white sand extends along the ocean for seven kilometres, palm-lined and so soft that you think you are lying in cotton wool. During the day you gaze at pure aquamarine, in the evening at a gently tinted play of colours with which the sun fades into the ocean. If you turn your gaze inland, you see nature in all of the green tones of a painter's palette merging with the houses, as well as people with a friendly, shy smile in their eyes – and the Evason Ana Mandara Resort. In the style of a typical Vietnamese village, the hotel is situated in the midst of a tropical garden, is furnished with local wood, rattan and light-coloured fabrics, has shady boardwalks on which the sand crunches, open verandas and one of the most respected spas in the country. Beneath coconut palms and with the quiet murmur of the sea and waterfalls in the background, one relaxes here with massages in the open-air sala, under the Vichy shower or in the Japanese-inspired bath. Within just a few hours the tensions of a whole year dissolve into pleasure – the newly won energy can later be used for an excursion to one of the small islands off of Nha Trang, a diving trip or a drive to the nearby Bao Dai Villa. This is where Bao Dai, Vietnam's last emperor, spent his summers – with a dazzling view of the city, the sparkling water and a view to the horizon where, even then, the sun was already setting in such a cinematic way.

Book to pack: "The Moon Bamboo" by Thich Nhat Hanh

Evason Ana Mandara Resort
Beachside Tran Phu Boulevard
Nha Trang, Vietnam
Tel. +84 (58) 352 22 22
Fax +84 (58) 352 58 28
Email: reservations-nhatrang@sixsenses.com
Website: www.sixsenses.com
www.great-escapes-hotels.com

DIRECTIONS	Situated 450 km/280 miles northeast of Ho Chi Minh City and 2 km/1.2 miles from Nha Trang (15 minute drive to the airport).
RATES	$$$
ROOMS	32 Garden View Rooms, 8 Sea View Rooms, 24 Deluxe Rooms and 4 Ana Mandara Suites.
FOOD	Vietnamese dishes and ambitious East-meets-West menus.
HISTORY	Opened in September 1997.
X-FACTOR	Relax in one of Vietnam's best spas.

Von Natur aus schön

Am Strand von Nha Trang zeigt sich Vietnam von seiner
Hochglanzseite. Über sieben Kilometer zieht sich der weiße
Sand am Ozean entlang, palmengesäumt und so weich, dass
man meint, in Watte zu liegen. Tagsüber fällt der Blick auf
reines Aquamarin, abends auf ein weichgezeichnetes Farbspiel, mit dem die Sonne im Meer verglüht. Wer in Richtung
Land schaut, sieht die Natur in sämtlichen Grüntönen des
Malkastens auf Tuchfühlung mit den Häusern gehen,
Menschen mit einem freundlich-schüchternen Lächeln in
den Augen – und das Evason Ana Mandara Resort. Im Stil
eines typisch vietnamesischen Dorfes liegt das Hotel inmitten eines tropischen Gartens, ist mit einheimischen Hölzern,
Rattan und hellen Stoffen ausgestattet, besitzt schattige
boardwalks, auf denen der Sand knirscht, offene Veranden
und eines der angesehensten Spas des Landes. Unter Kokos-
palmen und mit dem leisen Rauschen von Meer und Wasserfällen im Hintergrund entspannt man hier bei Massagen in
der Open-air-Sala, unter der Vichy-Dusche oder im japanisch
angehauchten Bad. Innerhalb weniger Stunden lösen sich
die Verspannungen eines ganzen Jahres in Genuss auf – die
neu gewonnene Energie wird später für den Ausflug auf
eine der kleinen Inseln vor Nha Trang genutzt, einen Tauch-
gang oder die Fahrt zur nahen Bao Dai Villa. Dort verbrachte
Vietnams letzter König Bao Dai seine Sommerfrische – mit
Traumblick auf die Stadt, das glitzernde Wasser und einem
Horizont, an dem die Sonne schon damals so kinotauglich
unterging.

Buchtipp: »Der Mondbambus« von Thich Nhat Hanh

Une beauté naturelle

La plage de Nha Trang est l'une des plus belles du Viêt-nam.
Bordée de palmiers, elle s'étire sur sept kilomètres le long
de l'océan, et le sable est si blanc et si doux que l'on a l'impression de marcher sur de la ouate. Le jour les vagues ont
une teinte aigue-marine, le soir une symphonie de couleurs
floues s'élève pendant que le soleil embrase la mer. Celui
qui regarde en direction des terres voit la végétation dans
une superbe palette de verts se marier aux habitations, des
gens timides et souriants et l' Evason Ana Mandara Resort.
Edifié dans le style d'un village traditionnel vietnamien,
l'hôtel est situé dans un vaste jardin tropical. L'intérieur
fait la part belle aux bois régionaux, au rotin et aux étoffes
claires. Il possède des caillebotis ombragés sur lesquels le
sable crisse, des vérandas ouvertes et un des centres de remise en forme les plus renommés du pays. Sous les cocotiers et avec en fond sonore le doux grondement de la mer
et des cascades, on se détend ici en se faisant masser en
plein air, sous la douche Vichy ou dans la salle de bains
aux accents nippons.

En l'espace de quelques heures, les tensions accumulées
pendant toute l'année cèdent la place au plaisir. Ce regain
d'énergie sera utile plus tard durant l'excursion sur une des
petites îles qui se trouvent devant Nha Trang, pour aller faire
de la plongée ou se rendre en voiture jusqu'à la villa de Bao
Dai. C'est là en effet, que le dernier empereur du Viêt-nam
se réfugiait durant les grandes chaleurs. Il avait d'ici une vue
superbe sur la ville, sur l'eau scintillante et sur les couchers
de soleil que le cinéma n'avait pas encore découvert.

**Livre à emporter : « La plénitude de l'instant » de Thich Nhat
Hanh**

ANREISE	450 km nordöstlich von Ho Chi Minh City gelegen und 2 km von Nha Trang entfernt (15-minütige Fahrt zum Flughafen).
PREIS	$$$
ZIMMER	32 Gardenview Rooms, 8 Seaview Rooms, 24 Deluxe Rooms und 4 Ana-Mandara-Suiten.
KÜCHE	Vietnamesische Gerichte und ambitionierte East-meets-West-Menüs.
GESCHICHTE	Im September 1997 eröffnet.
X-FAKTOR	Eines der besten Spas in Vietnam.

ACCÈS	A 450 km au nord-est de Ho Chi Minh City et à 2 km de Nha Trang (15 min en voiture jusqu'à l'aéroport).
PRIX	$$$
CHAMBRES	32 Gardenview Rooms, 8 Seaview Rooms, 24 Deluxe Rooms et 4 Ana Mandara Suites.
RESTAURATION	Cuisine vietnamienne et menus East-meets-West.
HISTOIRE	Ouvert depuis septembre 1997.
LE « PETIT PLUS »	Un des plus beaux centres de remise en forme du Viêt-nam.

On Mao's Trail...
Red Capital Club & Residence, Beijing

On Mao's Trail

The impression you get in the Chairman's Suite is that Mao has only just left the building. Black-and-white photos of his family hang on the wall; his favourite books fill the shelves and an Art Deco lamp from his house in Zhongnanhai adorns one corner. It is almost a disappointment when the doors open and the man who was once China's most power-ful leader does not walk back into the room. But despite his absence, the Red Capital Club still exudes the complete com-munist flair of the 1950s. The house in Beijing's Dongsi quarter is in the style of the private residences which were sought after by leading politicians after 1949 as their pieds-à-terre of choice, and the five suites are furnished in impres-sive detail. The concubines' rooms are to the right and left of the Chairman's Suite; they seem to consist almost entire-ly of beds and are furnished with antiques from the Qing Dynasty. Two other suites are dedicated to the Chinese writer Han Suiyin and Edgar Snow respectively. The former political elite of the country also makes an appearance in the restaurant whose "Zhongnanhai cuisine" includes Mao's favourite dishes. Even when embarking on excursions into the city, you follow in Mao's tracks. Or to put it more accu-rately, in his tracks – because the stretch-limousine that once used to chauffeur Madame Mao and which is the only exist-ing car of this type left, is today available for the exclusive use of hotel guests. All seven metres of it including red flags, champagne and Russian caviar.

Book to pack: "The Private Life of Chairman Mao: The Memoirs of Mao's Personal Physician" by Li Zhi-Sui

Red Capital Club & Residence
No. 9 Dongsi Liutiao
Dongcheng District
Beijing 100007, China
Tel. +86 (10) 840 353 08
Fax +86 (10) 840 353 03
Email: info@redcapitalclub.com.cn
Website: www.redcapitalclub.com.cn
www.great-escapes-hotels.com

DIRECTIONS	Situated in Beijing's Dongsi quarter, 30 minutes from the airport.
RATES	$$
ROOMS	2 Author's Suites, 2 Concubine's Suites, 1 Chairman's Suite.
FOOD	"Zhongnanhai cuisine". In other words: Mao's favourite foods and everything that was once served up at state banquets.
HISTORY	This former residence for leading politicians has been a small hotel since 1 July 2001.
X-FACTOR	Living like the socialist political elite.

Auf Maos Spuren

Die Chairman's Suite wirkt, als hätte Mao nur eben kurz den Raum verlassen – an der Wand hängen Schwarz-Weiß-Aufnahmen seiner Familie, im Regal stehen seine Lieblingsbücher und eine Ecke ziert eine Art-déco-Lampe aus seinem Haus in Zhongnanhai. Man ist fast enttäuscht, wenn die Türe aufgeht und nicht der einst mächtigste Mann Chinas ins Zimmer zurückkehrt; doch der Red Capital Club verbreitet auch ohne ihn das vollendet kommunistische Flair der fünfziger Jahre. Das Haus im Dongsi-Viertel von Peking knüpft an die Tradition der Privatresidenzen an, die sich führende Politiker nach 1949 als bevorzugte Adressen aussuchten, und hat fünf Suiten, die mit unvorstellbarer Liebe zum Detail eingerichtet sind. Rechts und links der Chairman's Suite liegen die Zimmer der Konkubinen, die fast nur aus Betten zu bestehen scheinen und für die man Antiquitäten aus der Qing-Dynastie auftrieb. Zwei weitere Suiten wurden dem chinesischen Schriftsteller Han Suiyin sowie Edgar Snow gewidmet. Präsent ist die einstige politische Elite des Landes auch im Restaurant, hinter dessen »Zhongnanhai Cuisine« sich die Lieblingsgerichte Maos verbergen, und selbst Ausflüge durch die Stadt unternimmt man auf Maos Spuren. Besser gesagt, in seiner Spur – denn die sieben Meter lange Stretch-Limousine, in der sich Madame Mao chauffieren ließ und die der einzige noch existierende Wagen dieses Typs ist, steht heute exklusiv den Gästen des Hauses zur Verfügung. Inklusive roter Flagge, Champagner und russischem Kaviar.

Buchtipp: »Ich war Maos Leibarzt« von Zhi-Sui Li

Sur les traces de Mao

En pénétrant dans la suite présidentielle, on a l'impression que Mao vient juste de quitter la pièce : des photographies en noir et blanc de sa famille sont encore accrochées au mur, ses livres préférés reposent sur l'étagère et une lampe Art déco provenant de sa maison à Zhongnanhai orne un coin de la salle. Quand la porte s'ouvre, on est presque déçu de ne pas se retrouver face à l'homme qui fut, à son époque, le plus puissant de la Chine. Pourtant, même en l'absence de celui-ci, l'atmosphère du communisme des années cinquante plane encore sur le Red Capital Club. La maison située dans le quartier Dongsi de Pékin se rattache à la tradition des résidences privées, particulièrement prisées des hommes politiques à partir de 1949. Ses cinq suites sont aménagées avec un amour du détail particulièrement étonnant. A droite et à gauche de la suite présidentielle se trouvent les chambres des concubines qui semblent n'être composées que de lits et pour lesquelles on dénicha des antiquités de la dynastie des Qing. Deux autres suites ont été dédiées à l'écrivain chinois Han Suyin et à Edgar Snow. Le grand timonier est également présent dans la salle de restaurant puisque la « Zhongnanhai Cuisine » propose ses plats préférés. Même lors des excursions à travers la ville, il convient de partir sur les traces de Mao. Ou à la place de ce dernier, devrait-on dire, car la longue limousine de sept mètres, qui servait jadis aussi à Madame Mao et qui est la seule automobile de ce type à exister encore, se tient exclusivement à la disposition des clients de la maison. Petit drapeau rouge, champagne et caviar russe compris.

Livre à emporter : « La vie privée du président Mao »
de Zhi-Sui Li

ANREISE	Im Dongsi-Viertel Pekings gelegen, 30 Fahrtminuten vom Flughafen entfernt.
PREIS	$$
ZIMMER	2 Author's-Suiten, 2 Concubine's-Suiten, 1 Chairman's-Suite.
KÜCHE	»Zhongnanhai Cuisine«. Übersetzt: Maos Leibspeisen und alles, was einst bei Staatsbanketten auf den Tisch kam.
GESCHICHTE	Die ehemalige Residenz führender Politiker ist seit 1. Juli 2001 ein kleines Hotel.
X-FAKTOR	Wohnen wie die politische Elite des Sozialismus.

ACCÈS	Situé dans le quartier Dongsi de Pékin à 30 min en voiture de l'aéroport.
PRIX	$$
CHAMBRES	2 Author's suites, 2 Concubine's suites, 1 Chairman's suite.
RESTAURATION	« Zhongnanhai Cuisine » : les plats préférés de Mao et tous les plats servis lors des banquets de l'Etat.
HISTOIRE	Depuis le 1er juillet 2001, l'ancienne résidence des personnalités politiques est devenue un petit hôtel.
LE « PETIT PLUS »	Résider comme l'élite politique à l'époque du communisme.

New Perspectives in Ancient C

Commune by the Great Wall, Beijing

Commune by the Great Wall, Beijing

New Perspectives in Ancient China

It is every architect's dream commission: To build a house in a world-famous environment and entirely according to one's own ideas – and only with one guiding principle: that it inspires a whole generation and a whole continent. For 12 architects from Asia, this dream has become a reality of concrete, glass and wood. In Shuiguan Valley, north of Peking and on a plot of land directly by the Great Wall, they designed the Commune by the Great Wall. Their villas are situated in the midst of green hills far from the tourist hubbub and bear no relation whatsoever to what is usually celebrated as "modern architecture" in China. For example, in his Furniture House, Shigeru Ban of Japan experiments with bamboo plywood and situates the more than minimally furnished rooms around a glassed-off inner courtyard. With the Cantilever House, Antonio Ochoa, a Venezuelan who emigrated to China, adheres to the principle of simple geometry and almost brutally places his building of concrete, cement and red brick in the gentle landscape. And Kanika R'kul of Thailand designed the Shared House, which is set up as a type of educational weekend house. With the help of light and space, terraces and inner courtyards, it is intended to prepare its urban residents for life in the country. Critics of the Commune by the Great Wall find fault with the occasional bad materials and building quality as well as with a certain naïveté, but the grounds are nonetheless considered one of the most creative and courageous private architecture projects in China. In 2002, it won the special prize at the Biennial in Venice and also recently became a member of the Design Hotels, since the villas are not only exhibits, but luxury residences for fans of avant-garde Asian architecture as well.

Book to pack: "Red Azalea" by Anchee Min

Commune by the Great Wall	
Exit at Shuiguan	
Badaling Highway	
Beijing 102102, China	
Tel. + 86 (10) 81 18–18 88	
Fax + 86 (10) 81 18–18 66	
Email: reservation@commune.com.cn	
Website: www.commune.com.cn and	
www.designhotels.com	
www.great-escapes-hotels.com	

DIRECTIONS	Situated in Shuiguan Valley 60 km/37 miles north of Beijing.
RATES	$$$
ROOMS	Currently there are 24 villas, each with a private butler. When it is completed, there should be 59 guesthouses.
FOOD	Breakfast is served in the villas and lunch and dinner in the clubhouse restaurant. Creative Chinese cuisine and international menus.
HISTORY	Private project of SOHO China Ltd.
X-FACTOR	A successful experiment.

Neue Perspektiven im alten China

Es ist eine Aufgabe, von der jeder Architekt träumt: Ein Haus in einer weltberühmten Umgebung und ganz nach eigenen Vorstellungen zu bauen – nur unter der Vorgabe, mit ihm eine ganze Generation und einen ganzen Kontinent zu inspirieren. Für zwölf Architekten aus Asien ist dieser Traum zu einer Realität aus Beton, Glas und Holz geworden – sie haben im Shuiguan-Tal nördlich von Peking und auf einem Grundstück direkt an der Großen Mauer die Commune by the Great Wall entworfen. Ihre Villen stehen weitab vom Touristentrubel inmitten grüner Hügel und haben mit dem, was in China sonst als »moderne Architektur« gefeiert wird, so gar nichts zu tun. Shigeru Ban aus Japan zum Beispiel experimentiert in seinem Furniture House mit Sperrholz aus Bambus und legt die mehr als minimalistisch möblierten Zimmer rund um einen verglasten Innenhof an; Antonio Ochoa, ein nach China ausgewanderter Venezolaner, verschreibt sich mit dem Cantilever House ganz dem Prinzip der *simple geometry* und drückt sein Gebäude aus Beton, Zement und rotem Backstein fast brutal in die sanfte Landschaft. Und von Kanika R'kul (Thailand) stammt der Entwurf zum The Shared House, das als eine Art erziehendes Wochenendhaus angelegt ist und seine Bewohner mit Hilfe von Licht und Raum, Terrassen und Innenhöfen vom Stadt- aufs Landleben vorbereiten soll. Die Kritiker dieser Commune by the Great Wall bemängeln eine teils schlechte Material- und Bauqualität sowie eine gewisse Weltferne – doch trotzdem zählt die Anlage zu den kreativsten und mutigsten privaten Architekturprojekten in China. 2002 gewann sie den Sonderpreis auf der Biennale von Venedig und ist seit kurzem Mitglied der design hotels; denn die Villen sind nicht nur Exponate, sondern auch Luxusresidenzen für Fans avantgardistischer asiatischer Architektur.

Buchtipp: »Rote Azalee« von Anchee Min

Perspectives nouvelles pour la Chine ancienne

Tous les architectes rêvent de se voir confier cette tâche : construire la maison qu'ils désirent sur un site célèbre dans le monde entier – seule condition : donner des idées à une génération et à tout un continent. Ce rêve s'est concrétisé en béton, en verre et en bois pour les douze architectes asiatiques qui ont créé la Commune by the Great Wall dans la vallée de Shuiguan, au nord de Pékin et à proximité de la Grande Muraille.

Ses villas se dressent au milieu de collines verdoyantes, loin des afflux de touristes, et n'ont absolument rien de commun avec ce que les Chinois fêtent sous le nom d'« architecture moderne ». Le Japonais Shigeru Ban, par exemple, expérimente le contreplaqué en bambou dans sa Furniture House et agence les pièces meublées avec un minimalisme strict autour d'un atrium vitré ; la Cantilever House d'Antonio Ochoa, un Vénézuélien immigré en Chine, est vouée entièrement au principe de la géométrie simple et l'édifice en béton, ciment et briques rouges est posé presque brutalement dans le doux paysage. Quant à The Shared House de Kanika R'kul, originaire de Thaïlande, elle est aménagée comme une maison de week-end éducative et doit préparer les citadins à vivre à la campagne à l'aide de lumière et d'espace, de terrasses et de cours intérieures.

Les critiques reprochent à The Commune by the Great Wall la qualité de ses matériaux et de la construction qui laisse en partie à désirer ainsi qu'un certain éloignement du monde. N'empêche que le complexe fait partie des projets d'architecture privés les plus créatifs et les plus courageux en Chine. Il a remporté le prix spécial de la Biennale de Venise en 2002 et fait depuis peu partie des hôtels design. C'est que les villas ne sont pas seulement des objets d'exposition mais aussi des résidences de luxe pour les amoureux de l'architecture asiatique d'avant-garde.

Livre à emporter : « L'azalée rouge » d'Anchee Min

ANREISE	Im Shuiguan-Tal 60 km nördlich von Peking gelegen.
PREIS	$$$
ZIMMER	Gegenwärtig 24 Villen mit jeweils privatem Butler. Nach Abschluss aller Arbeiten sollen es 59 Gästehäuser sein.
KÜCHE	Frühstück in den Villen, Lunch und Dinner im Clubhaus-Restaurant. Kreative chinesische Küche und internationale Menüs.
GESCHICHTE	Privates Projekt der SOHO China Ltd.
X-FAKTOR	Ein gelungenes Experiment.

ACCÈS	Située dans la vallée du Shuiguan, à 60 km au nord de Pékin.
PRIX	$$$
CHAMBRES	Actuellement 24 villas avec majordome particulier. Elles seront 59 après l'achèvement des travaux.
RESTAURATION	Le petit-déjeuner est servi dans les villas, le déjeuner et le dîner au Club-Restaurant. Cuisine chinoise innovante et menus internationaux.
HISTOIRE	Projet privé de la SOHO China Ltd.
LE « PETIT PLUS »	Une expérience réussie.

A Glowing Example...
Gôra Kadan, Gôra

Gôra Kadan, Gôra

A Glowing Example

It is rare for a mountain to look so gentle. Mount Fuji lies there with slopes so soft that it looks as though it were made not of rocks, but a pile of green-brown sand, that a giant hand had let trickle to the ground and then sprinkled with snow crystals. But Japan's sacred peak is a total challenge. It only permits the approach of hikers in July and August and if you wish to experience a sunrise here, you have to bring warm clothing, stamina and a predilection for over-filled mattress facilities. It is well worth considering doing without the multi-coloured dawn spectacle and taking the hundred times more relaxed route – in the Gôra Kadan for example. This fairytale-like house can be found in Hakone National Park surrounded by trees whose outlines are so sharp that they look like colourful paper cut-outs and classic templates for clarity and symmetry. The imperial family once spent its summer weekends here. Since 1952 the Gôra Kadan has been a hotel; with typical Tatami mats, cypress baths and a lighting design that could compete with the best theatre stages in the world. A shimmering lantern here, five lamps there, which cast sparkling gold beams of light on the stone path, and over the pool a paned glass roof that conjures rainbows out of sunbeams. It is a condensation of Japanese serenity – still situated within the energy field of the Fuji, but far from the hurly-burly around the sugar-powdered peak.

Book to pack: "Naokos Smile" by Haruki Murakami

Gôra Kadan
1300 Gôra
Hakone – Machi, Ashigara – Shimogun
Kanagawa-ken 250-0408
Tel. +81 (460) 233 31
Fax +81 (460) 233 34
Email: spa@gorakadan.com
Website: www.gorakadan.com
www.great-escapes-hotels.com

DIRECTIONS	Situated 90 km/56 miles southwest of Tokyo (city centre), 170 km/106 miles from Tokyo-Narita Airport.
RATES	$$$$
ROOMS	38 rooms including 12 suites.
FOOD	Traditional Kaiseki cuisine; almost too beautiful too eat.
HISTORY	Formerly the imperial summer residence, opened as a hotel in 1952 and renovated in 1989.
X-FACTOR	Tranquillity itself – surrounded by fabulous nature.

Ein leuchtendes Beispiel

Selten sieht ein Berg so sanft aus. Der Fuji liegt mit seinen weichen Flanken da, als wäre er nicht aus Fels gemacht, sondern bloß ein Haufen grünbrauner Sand, den eine Riesenhand zu Boden rieseln ließ und mit Schneekristallen bestreut hat. Doch Japans heiliger Gipfel ist durchaus eine Herausforderung. Nur im Juli und August erlaubt er Wanderern, sich ihm zu nähern – wer hier einen Sonnenaufgang erleben möchte, muss warme Kleidung, Kondition und ein Faible für überfüllte Matratzenlager mitbringen. Da ist es eine Überlegung wert, auf das morgendliche Farbspiel zu verzichten und dafür hundertfach entspannter zu logieren – im Gôra Kadan etwa. Das märchenhafte Haus steht im Nationalpark von Hakone, um sich herum nur Bäume, deren Konturen so scharf gezeichnet sind, als wären es bunte Scherenschnitte und Musterbeispiele an Klarheit und Symmetrie. Einst verbrachte die kaiserliche Familie hier ihre Sommerwochenenden – seit 1952 ist das Gôra Kadan ein Hotel mit typischen Tatami-Matten, Zypressenbädern und einer Lichtdramaturgie, die den besten Theaterbühnen der Erde Konkurrenz machen könnte. Hier eine schimmernde Laterne, dort fünf Lampen, die goldglänzende Kegel auf den Steinweg werfen, und über dem Pool ein kassettenartiges Glasdach, das aus Sonnenstrahlen einen Regenbogen zaubert. Es ist ein Konzentrat des stillen Japan – noch im Energiefeld des Fuji gelegen, aber weit weg vom Trubel rund um den Puderzuckergipfel.
Buchtipp: »Naokos Lächeln« von Haruki Murakami

Calme et lumière

Rares sont les montagnes qui ont l'air aussi peu menaçantes. Le Fuji-yama aux doux versants ne donne pas l'impression d'être fait de pierres et de roches, mais d'être un tas de sable vert-brun qu'une main de géant aurait fait ruisseler sur le sol et poudré de cristaux de neige. Pourtant l'ascension de la montagne sacrée du Japon n'en représente pas moins un défi. Ce n'est que durant les mois de juillet et d'août qu'il permet aux promeneurs de l'approcher – celui qui veut assister ici au lever du soleil, doit apporter des vêtements chauds, jouir d'une bonne condition physique et avoir un faible pour les campement surpeuplés. A tout prendre, mieux vaut peut-être renoncer à ce flamboiement des couleurs matinal et prendre ses aises au Gôra Kadan par exemple. Ressemblant à une maison de conte de fées, l'hôtel est situé dans le parc national de Harkone. Exemple de clarté et de symétrie, il est entouré d'arbres aux contours si nets qu'on les croirait découpés au ciseau. Jadis la famille impériale y venait durant l'été passer les fins de semaine. Depuis 1952, le Gôra Kadan est un hôtel traditionnel avec tatamis, cuves de cyprès et une dramaturgie de la lumière qui pourrait entrer en compétition avec les meilleures scènes de théâtre du monde entier. Ici la lueur tremblotante d'une lanterne, là les boules d'or que dessinent cinq lampes sur le chemin de pierre, et, au-dessus de la piscine, un toit de verre en cassettes qui métamorphose les rayons du soleil en arc en ciel. L'hôtel reflète toute la sérénité du Japon et s'il se trouve encore dans le champ d'énergie du Fuji-yama, il est à mille lieux de toute cette agitation qui règne autour de lui.
Livre à emporter : « Au sud de la frontière, à l'ouest du soleil » de Haruki Murakami

ANREISE	90 km südwestlich von Tokio (Stadtzentrum) gelegen, 170 km vom Flughafen Tokio-Narita entfernt.
PREIS	$$$$
ZIMMER	38 Zimmer, darunter 12 Suiten.
KÜCHE	Traditionelle Kaiseki-Küche; fast zu schön zum Aufessen.
GESCHICHTE	Einst der kaiserliche Sommersitz, 1952 als Hotel eröffnet und 1989 renoviert.
X-FAKTOR	Die Ruhe selbst – inmitten einer traumhaften Natur.

ACCÈS	Situé à 90 km au sud-ouest de Tokyo (centre) et à 170 km de l'aéroport de Tokyo-Narita.
PRIX	$$$$
CHAMBRES	38 chambres, dont 12 suites.
RESTAURATION	Cuisine kaiseki traditionnelle ; si belle qu'on hésite à la consommer.
HISTOIRE	Résidence d'été impériale, l'hôtel a ouvert ses portes en 1952 et a été rénové en 1989.
LE « PETIT PLUS »	Le calme dans une nature enchanteresse.

The Fount of Knowledge...
Asaba, Shizuoka-ken

The Fount of Knowledge

There are these photos with three or four men sitting in a steaming Japanese pool and somehow they manage to look both bored and extremely pleased. Since they are mostly somewhat advanced in years, you get the impression that you would have to spend your entire life training for such a facial expression – but sometimes just a few days are all you need. For example, on the peninsula of Izu where Japan's oldest thermal springs bubble and the Hotel Asaba was already accommodating spa guests long before the term "wellness oasis" was invented. In 1675 the Asaba family opened their small house in the midst of a bamboo forest and on the banks of a pool upon whose surface the building almost seems to float. Today, as in the past, what counts here are clear design, simple forms and colours – they supplement the surrounding nature which looks like it has been softly sketched and bring out its mysticism perfectly. Rugged rocks from the region surround the outer pool; the rooms and baths are also furnished with local materials, and from every room you have a view of the surrounding vegetation. If the natural spectacle is not enough for you, then attend a theatre evening on the floating stage – the traditional dances and lyrical dramas beneath a star-studded sky are magical. And after a few days you will have attained that pleasant, celestial state – as proof, a single photo is all that you will need. The photo will show a person who looks both bored and extremely pleased.

Book to pack: "The Dancing Girl of Izu" by Yasunari Kawabata, "Memoirs of a Geisha" by Arthur Golden

Asaba
3450–1 Shuzenji-Machi
Shizuoka-ken 410–2416
Japan
Tel. +81 (558) 72 70 00
Fax +81 (558) 72 70 77
Email: asaba@relaischateaux.com
Website: www.relaischateaux.com
www.great-escapes-hotels.com

DIRECTIONS	Situated in the north of the peninsula of Izu, 200 km/124 miles southwest of Tokyo-Narita Airport.
RATES	$$$$
ROOMS	15 rooms, 4 suites.
FOOD	Traditional Japanese dishes prepared from regional ingredients.
HISTORY	Opened in 1675 as a small inn and has been one of the most beautiful thermal hotels in Japan ever since.
X-FACTOR	Where simple hot water equals happiness.

Die Quelle der Erkenntnis

Es gibt diese Bilder, auf denen drei oder vier Männer in einem dampfenden japanischen Becken sitzen und es irgendwie schaffen, zugleich gelangweilt und ungeheuer zufrieden dreinzuschauen. Ihr meist etwas höheres Alter lässt den Eindruck entstehen, man müsse für diesen Gesichtsausdruck ein Leben lang trainieren – dabei genügen manchmal wenige Tage. Zum Beispiel auf der Halbinsel Izu, wo die ältesten Thermalquellen Japans sprudeln und das Hotel Asaba schon Kurgäste empfing, als der Begriff Wellness-Oase noch gar nicht erfunden war: 1675 eröffnete die Familie Asaba das kleine Haus inmitten eines Bambuswaldes und am Ufer eines Teichs, über dessen Wasserfläche die Gebäude fast zu schweben scheinen. Damals wie heute zählen hier klares Design, einfache Formen und Farben – sie ergänzen die umliegende Natur, die stets wie weichgezeichnet wirkt, und bringen ihre Mystik perfekt zur Geltung. Unbearbeitete Felsen aus der Gegend umrahmen die Außenbecken, auch die Zimmer und Bäder sind mit einheimischen Materialien ausgestattet, und man blickt von jedem Raum aus ins Grüne. Wem das natürliche Schauspiel nicht genügt, der besucht einen Theaterabend auf der schwimmenden Bühne – die traditionellen Tänze und Singspiele unterm Sternenhimmel sind Magie. Und nach ein paar Tagen hat man dann jenen angenehmen, gleichsam sphärischen Zustand erreicht, für dessen Beweis ein einziges Foto genügt: Das Bild zeigt einen Menschen, der zugleich gelangweilt und ungeheuer zufrieden dreinschaut.

Buchtipps: »Die Tänzerin von Izu« von Yasunari Kawabata, »Die Geisha« von Arthur Golden

Aux sources de la félicité

Qui ne connaît pas ces photos sur lesquelles on peut voir, assis dans un bain de vapeur japonais, trois ou quatre hommes, dont les visages expriment à la fois l'ennui et un contentement suprême ? Puisqu'ils sont en général d'un grand âge, on peut être amené à penser qu'ils ont dû s'exercer toute leur vie pour obtenir cette expression particulière – mais parfois quelques jours seulement suffisent. Par exemple sur l'archipel d'Izu où jaillissent les plus anciennes sources thermales du Japon et où l'hôtel Asaba accueillait déjà des curistes alors que le mot « wellness » n'existait pas encore. C'est en 1675 que la famille Asaba ouvrit la petite maison située au milieu d'une forêt de bambous et au bord d'un étang au-dessus duquel les bâtiments paraissent presque flotter. Aujourd'hui comme hier le design sobre, les formes simples et les couleurs sont de la plus haute importance – ils complètent la nature environnante, dont les contours semblent toujours quelque peu estompés, et mettent parfaitement en valeur son côté mystique. Des rochers non travaillés provenant des environs encadrent les bassins extérieurs, les chambres et les salles de bains sont décorées avec des matériaux de la région, et chaque pièce offre une vue sur la verdure. Celui qui ne peut se contenter de ce spectacle de la nature, ira à une soirée théâtrale donnée sur la scène flottante – les danses et les pièces chantées traditionnelles sont magiques sous le ciel étoilé. Au bout de quelques jours, on atteint alors cet état de félicité et la photo prise à ce moment montre un visage à la fois ennuyé et extrêmement satisfait.

Livres à emporter : « La Danseuse d'Izu » de Yasunari Kawabata, « Geisha » de Arthur Golden

ANREISE	Im Norden der Halbinsel Izu gelegen, 200 km südwestlich des Flughafens Tokio-Narita.
PREIS	$$$$
ZIMMER	15 Zimmer, 4 Suiten.
KÜCHE	Klassische japanische Gerichte aus regionalen Zutaten.
GESCHICHTE	1675 als kleines Gasthaus eröffnet und seitdem eines der schönsten Thermenhotels in Japan.
X-FAKTOR	Wo einfaches heißes Wasser glücklich macht.

ACCÈS	Situé au nord de l'archipel d'Izu, à 200 km au sud-ouest de l'aéroport de Tokyo-Narita.
PRIX	$$$$
CHAMBRES	15 chambres, 4 suites
RESTAURATION	Plats japonais classiques préparés avec des produits de la région.
HISTOIRE	Petite auberge ouverte en 1675, elle est devenue l'un des plus beaux hôtels thermaux du Japon.
LE « PETIT PLUS »	Incroyable comme un peu d'eau chaude peut rendre heureux.

On Form...
Benesse House, Naoshima

On Form

Art in hotels is often something which one notes upon arrival with slight irritation and hopefully quickly forgets after departure. There are few houses which provide the proper context for pictures or sculptures, and even fewer houses which themselves become works of art. One of these rare exceptions is the Benesse House on the island of Naoshima, designed by Tadao Ando in 1992. The Japanese star architect does not even attempt to compete with the Zen surroundings – sparkling blue water, radiant green vegetation and a stillness that one can hear – but instead counters nature's beauties with concrete, marble, glass and steel in precisely demarcated geometric forms and clear lines. More than half of the building's surface is spread underground and nonetheless permits so much light, space and expanse in a way that many penthouses cannot compete with. The Benesse House, which from the air looks like a giant Fisher-Price toy, is linked to the galleries of the Naoshima Contemporary Art Museum. Its permanent collection is dedicated to the relationship between nature and humans and shows contemporary Japanese artists like Hiroshi Sugimoto with his "Seascape Series"; there are also fantastic exhibits like Bruce Nauman's blinking neon installation "100 Live and Die" in a huge concrete cylinder with a transom window. The concept does not stop at the restaurant and cafeteria; both are far from what one otherwise knows as museum rest stops and serve elaborate Kaiseki cuisine – menus have names like "Sound of the Ocean" or "Wind between the Pine Trees".

Book to pack: "The Woman in the Dunes" by Kobo Abe

Benesse House

Gotanji, Naoshima-cho, Kagawan-gun,
Kagawa, Japan 761-3110
Prefecture 761-3110, Japan
Tel. +81 (87) 892 20 30
Email: naoshima@mail.benesse.co.jp
Website: www.naoshima-is.co.jp
www.great-escapes-hotels.com

DIRECTIONS	Situated 30 km/19 miles north of Takamatsu in the inland sea (1.5 hr. by bus and ferry from Takamatsu Airport).
RATES	$$$
ROOMS	16 double rooms, all with various artworks and a view of the sea.
FOOD	Restaurant with first-class Kaiseki cuisine.
HISTORY	Designed by Tadao Ando in 1992; is both a hotel and museum.
X-FACTOR	The very best of art and architecture.

Gut in Form

Kunst im Hotel – das ist häufig etwas, was man bei der Ankunft leicht irritiert bemerkt und nach der Abreise hoffentlich schnell wieder vergisst. Nur selten gibt es Häuser, die Bildern oder Skulpturen den passenden Rahmen bieten, und noch viel seltener gibt es Häuser, die selbst zum Kunstwerk geworden sind. Eine dieser Ausnahmen ist das Benesse House auf der Insel Naoshima, das Tadao Ando 1992 entworfen hat. Der japanische Stararchitekt unternimmt erst gar keinen Versuch, mit der Zen-Umgebung – glitzernd blaues Wasser, grün leuchtende Vegetation und eine Stille, die man hören kann – zu konkurrieren, sondern setzt den Naturschönheiten Beton, Marmor, Glas und Stahl entgegen, wie ausgestanzte geometrische Formen und klare Linien. Mehr als die Hälfte der Gebäudefläche dehnt sich unterirdisch aus und vermittelt trotzdem so viel Licht, Raum und Weite wie es manches Penthouse nicht vermag. Verbunden ist das Benesse House, das aus der Luft betrachtet an ein riesiges Fisher-Price-Spielzeug erinnert, mit den Galerien des Naoshima Contemporary Art Museum. Dessen Dauerausstellung widmet sich den Beziehungen zwischen Natur und Mensch und zeigt zeitgenössische japanische Künstler wie Hiroshi Sugimoto mit seinen »Seascape Series«; fantastisch sind auch Exponate wie Bruce Naumans blinkende Neoninstallation »100 Live and Die« in einem gewaltigen Betonzylinder mit Oberlicht. Selbst vor dem Restaurant und der Cafeteria macht das Konzept nicht Halt. Beide Lokale sind weit entfernt von allem, was man sonst als museale Pausenstätten kennt und servieren kunstvolle Kaiseki-Küche – Menüs mit Titeln wie »Klang des Meeres« oder »Wind zwischen den Pinien«.

Buchtipp: »Die Frau in den Dünen« von Kobo Abe

La forme et le fond

Des objets d'art dans un hôtel – souvent on les remarque en arrivant avec une certaine irritation et on les oublie très vite le séjour terminé. Rares sont les maisons qui offrent aux tableaux et aux sculptures un cadre digne d'eux, plus rares encore celles qui sont devenues elles-mêmes des œuvres d'art. La Benesse House, dessinée par Tadao Ando en 1992 et située sur l'île de Naoshima, est de celles-là. L'architecte star japonais ne tente même pas de rivaliser avec l'environnement – eau bleue scintillante, végétation luxuriante et silence audible –, non, il confronte les beautés de la nature au béton, au marbre, au verre et à l'acier, à des formes géométriques et des lignes nettes.

Plus de la moitié de la surface construite se déploie en sous-sol, ce qui n'empêche pas le bâtiment d'offrir plus de lumière et d'espace que maint penthouse. La Benesse House, qui ressemble vue du ciel à un énorme jouet Fisher-Price, est reliée aux galeries du Musée d'Art contemporain de Naoshima dont l'exposition permanente est consacrée aux relations entre la nature et l'être humain. Des artistes japonais contemporains exposent ici leurs œuvres, tels Hiroshi Sugimoto avec ses « Seascapes Series » ou Bruce Nauman avec son installation néon scintillante « 100 Live and Die », placée dans un énorme cylindre en béton doté d'une verrière. Le restaurant et la cafétéria font également partie du concept. Ils sont à des années-lumière des bistros de musées tels qu'on les connaît aujourd'hui et servent une cuisine Kaiseki sophistiquée qui offre des menus au nom poétique comme « Le bruit de la mer » ou « Le vent entre les pins ».

Livre à emporter : « La femme des sables » de Kôbô Abé

ANREISE	30 km nördlich von Takamatsu in der Inlandsee gelegen (1,5h per Bus und Fähre vom Flughafen Takamatsu entfernt).
PREIS	$$$
ZIMMER	16 Doppelzimmer, alle mit verschiedenen Kunstwerken und Seeblick.
KÜCHE	Restaurant mit erstklassiger Kaiseki-Küche.
GESCHICHTE	1992 von Tadao Ando entworfen; Hotel und Museum zugleich.
X-FAKTOR	The very best of Art and Architecture.

ACCÈS	Situé à 30 km au nord de Takamatsu dans la Mer Intérieure (à 1 h ½ en autobus et en ferry de l'aéroport de Takamatsu).
PRIX	$$$
CHAMBRES	16 chambres doubles, abritant toutes des œuvres d'art et avec vue sur la mer.
RESTAURATION	Ue cuisine Kaiseki de première classe.
HISTOIRE	Ensemble architectural dessiné en 1992 par Tadao Ando.
LE « PETIT PLUS »	Le meilleur de l'art et de l'architecture.

› **absoluteasia.com**
Exclusive tours through Asia for the discriminating and well-heeled holidaymaker – deluxe educational trips, individually put together and including highlights such as trips to private art collections.

› **adventureindonesia.com**
A good address for the active holidaymaker with trekking tours through the highlands, destinations for cyclists and divers as well as survival training in the jungle.

› **allindiahotels.com**
Decide first which city you would like to visit, otherwise you will be confused by the number of hotels in India that can be booked on this page: Accommodation of all types on offer.

› **artoftravel.com**
Not very exciting in terms of graphics, but contains good advice for the real budget traveller: Trips for US$25 per day or less! Among things on the "syllabus" are: how to find low-priced plane tickets, how to find private guesthouses and how to protect your modest travel budget from pickpockets.

› **asiabookroom.com**
Specialising in literature from and about Asia – including out of print, second hand and antiquarian books.

› **asia-hotels.com**
A mega network with hotel offers and travel information on just about every Asian country, including maps and current tips.

› **asiantraveladventures.com**
In addition to the usual tours, this organizer offers moderate adventure holidays in Asia (for example, rafting in Nepal or kayaking in Thailand). A rare plus: the program also includes tours adapted to suit the needs of the disabled.

› **asiatours.net**
Well-suited for a preliminary overview: Trips though various Asian countries are offered. There are also extras like golf vacations in Thailand or cruises on the Andaman Sea.

› **boutiquelodging.com**
Small, privately run boutique hotels worldwide, with high standards in terms of style and service. Asia is represented with accommodation offers in China, Thailand, Cambodia, Java and Bali.

› **absoluteasia.com**
Exklusive Touren durch Asien für anspruchsvolle und gut betuchte Urlauber – Studienreisen de luxe, die individuell zusammengestellt werden und Highlights wie den Besuch privater Kunstsammlungen umfassen.

› **adventureindonesia.com**
Eine gute Adresse für Aktivurlauber: Mit Trekkingtouren durchs Hochland, Zielen für Radfahrer und Taucher sowie einem Überlebenstraining im Dschungel.

› **allindiahotels.com**
Zumindest die Stadt, die man besuchen möchte, sollte man vorher festlegen – sonst verwirrt die Menge an Hotels in Indien, die über diese Seite buchbar sind. Angeboten werden Häuser aller Kategorien.

› **artoftravel.com**
Grafisch eher unspektakulär, aber mit guten Ratschlägen für echte Budget-Traveler: Reisen für 25 $ pro Tag oder weniger! Auf dem »Lehrplan« steht unter anderem, wie man günstig an Flugtickets kommt, private Gasthäuser findet und sein geringes Reisebudget vor Taschendieben schützt.

› **asiabookroom.com**
Spezialisiert auf Literatur aus und über Asien – inklusive vergriffener Titel und antiquarischer Bücher.

› **asia-hotels.com**
Ein Mega-Netzwerk mit Hotelangeboten, Reiseinformationen über so gut wie jedes asiatische Land, samt Karten und aktuellen Tipps.

› **asiantraveladventures.com**
Neben den üblichen Rundreisen stellt dieser Veranstalter gemäßigten Abenteuerurlaub in Asien vor (zum Beispiel Rafting in Nepal oder Kajak fahren in Thailand). Seltener Pluspunkt: Auf dem Programm stehen auch behindertengerechte Touren.

› **asiatours.net**
Gut geeignet für den ersten Überblick: Angeboten werden Reisen durch diverse Länder Asiens, außerdem findet man Extras wie Golfurlaub in Thailand oder Segeltörns in der Andamanischen See.

› **boutiquelodging.com**
Privat geführte, kleine Boutiquehotels in aller Welt, die hohe Ansprüche an Stil und Service stellen. Asien ist mit Häusern in China, Thailand, Kambodscha, Java und Bali vertreten.

› **absoluteasia.com**
Des voyages en Asie sur mesure pour touristes exigeants qui ne regardent pas à la dépense – voyages culturels luxueux qui peuvent être organisés de manière individuelle et comprennent des points forts tels la visite de collections d'art particulières.

› **adventureindonesia.com**
Une bonne adresse pour les voyageurs actifs, qui offre des expéditions de trekking sur les plateaux, des circuits pour les cyclistes et des sites de plongée ainsi qu'un entraînement de survie dans la jungle.

› **allindiahotels.com**
Inscrire d'abord la destination choisie en Inde, sinon on est irrité par le nombre d'hôtels que l'on peut réserver sur ce site qui offre des maisons de toutes catégories.

› **artoftravel.com**
Peu spectaculaire sur le plan graphique mais offrant de bons conseils aux voyageurs qui veillent à leur budget avec des voyages à 25 $ par jour et moins encore! On y apprend par exemple comment acquérir des billets d'avion à tarif réduit, comment trouver des chambres chez l'habitant et comment protéger son pécule des voleurs en tout genre.

› **asiabookroom.com**
Sa spécialité : les auteurs asiatiques et les ouvrages sur l'Asie – titres en rupture de stock compris et antiquités.

› **asia-hotels.com**
Un réseau gigantesque offrant des informations sur les hôtels et les voyages dans pour ainsi dire tous les pays asiatiques avec des cartes et les tuyaux du moment.

› **asiantraveladventures.com**
A côté des circuits courants, ce site propose des séjours d'aventure à prix réduit en Asie (par exemple raft au Népal ou kayak en Thaïlande). Une qualité rare : offre des voyages réalisables par des personnes handicapées.

› **asiatours.net**
Bien fait pour le premier coup d'œil. Le site offre des voyages dans divers pays d'Asie ainsi que des extras comme un séjour-golf en Thaïlande ou un séjour-voile sur la mer d'Andaman.

TASCHEN Web Picks: Is your next vacation too far off? Then capture the magic of Asia on your computer screen at home with the help of these Web tips. Here you'll find even more Indian hotel palaces, Balinese dream villas and Malaysian beach bungalows,

› **chinavista.com**
Tips for lesser known sights and tours in China – also features eccentric souvenirs like a wine bottle cover made of dark green brocade and a chat room for travellers to China.

› **concierge.com**
Hotels on all continents, that have been recommended by "Condé Nast Traveller" with diverse rankings. There are also lots of tips for Asia, particularly for the cities of Singapore and Hong Kong.

› **discover-indonesia.com**
All-round offers with the most important flight schedules, car rental locations and hotels. There are also descriptions of sights and important festivals in Indonesia.

› **geckotravel.com**
A tour operator from England who specialises in Southeast Asia. Tours to Thailand, Laos, Cambodia, Vietnam and Malaysia are offered for groups and individual holidaymakers. There are also attractive last-minute offers.

› **heritagehotels.com**
This site presents more than 200 historical hotels (mainly in former palaces and forts) in India. You can also obtain information on safaris by jeep, horse or camel and even book them direct.

› **india-tourism.com**
The all-in-one offer for travellers to India – with maps, city guides, hotels and restaurants, news and events. For holidaymakers interested in culture, an overview of the museums and art galleries in the entire country is also provided.

› **indochina-services.com**
Good overview of Vietnam, Cambodia, Laos, Myanmar, Indonesia and Thailand including a databank of photos and links to the respective tourist information offices. Individual travellers also receive the addresses of select organizers.

› **jnto.go.jp**
Official site of the Japanese tourist office. Short, to the point and well organized – even the (excellent) road links within the country can be called up.

› **lonelyplanet.com**
Excellent online presentation by one of the world's best guidebook series. Also features comprehensive, current and critical information on all Asian destinations. So, for Myanmar, for example, the reasons to go and the reasons not to go are honestly listed.

› **chinavista.com**
Tipps für unbekanntere Sehenswürdigkeiten und Touren in China – außerdem mit exzentrischen Souvenirs wie einer Weinflaschenhülle aus dunkelgrünem Brokat sowie mit einem Chatroom für Chinareisende.

› **concierge.com**
Hotels auf allen Kontinenten, die der »Condé Nast Traveller« in diversen Rankings empfohlen hat. Zahlreiche Tipps auch für Asien, vor allem für die Metropolen Singapur und Hongkong.

› **discover-indonesia.com**
Allround-Angebot mit den wichtigsten Flugplänen, Stationen von Autovermietern und Hotels. Vorgestellt werden auch wichtige Festivals in Indonesien und Sehenswürdigkeiten.

› **geckotravel.com**
Ein Reiseveranstalter aus England, der sich auf Südostasien spezialisiert hat. Die Touren nach Thailand, Laos, Kambodscha, Vietnam und Malaysia werden für Gruppen- und Individualurlauber angeboten, außerdem gibt es attraktive Last-minute-Angebote.

› **heritagehotels.com**
Mehr als 200 historische Hotels (meist in ehemaligen Palästen und Forts) in Indien präsentieren sich auf diesen Seiten. Ferner kann man sich über Safaris per Jeep, Pferd oder Kamel informieren und auch gleich buchen.

› **india-tourism.com**
Das All-in-one-Angebot für Indienreisende. Mit Landkarten, Stadtführern, Hotels und Restaurants, Neuigkeiten und Events. Für Kultururlauber gibt es sogar eine Übersicht der Museen und Kunstgalerien im ganzen Land.

› **indochina-services.com**
Guter Überblick über Vietnam, Kambodscha, Laos, Indonesien, Thailand und Myanmar, inklusive Bilddatenbank und Links zu den jeweiligen Tourismusinformationsstellen. Individualreisende erhalten außerdem Adressen ausgewählter Veranstalter.

› **jnto.go.jp**
Offizielle Seite der Japanischen Fremdenverkehrszentrale. Kurz, knapp und gut durchorganisiert – sogar die (exzellenten) Verkehrsverbindungen innerhalb des Landes können abgerufen werden.

› **boutiquelodging.com**
Petits hôtels-boutiques privés dans le monde entier très exigeants sur le plan du style et du service. L'Asie y est représentée avec des maisons en Chine, en Thaïlande, au Cambodge à Java et Bali.

› **chinavista.com**
Tuyaux sur des sites intéressants moins connus et des circuits en Chine. Souvenirs excentriques tels une gaine de bouteille en brocart vert foncé et un chat-room destiné à ceux qui veulent visiter ou ont visité la Chine.

› **concierge.com**
Hôtels du monde entier, que le « Condé Nast Traveller » a recommandés dans divers classements. Nombreux tuyaux aussi sur l'Asie et surtout sur Singapour et Hong-Kong.

› **discover-indonesia.com**
Offre complète incluant les vols les plus importants, les endroits où trouver les locations de voiture et les hôtels. Présentation de grands festivals en Indonésie et de sites à ne pas manquer.

› **eckotravel.com**
Un tour-opérateur anglais aujourd'hui spécialiste du Sud-Est asiatique. Offre de voyages en groupes ou individuels en Thaïlande, au Laos, au Cambodge, au Viêt Nam et en Malaisie. Promotions intéressantes.

› **heritagehotels.com**
Présente plus de 200 hôtels historiques en Inde (situés le plus souvent dans d'anciens forts et des palais). Information sur des safaris en jeep, à cheval, à dos de chameau et possibilité de réservation immédiate.

› **india-tourism.com**
Le « tout en un » pour les voyageurs à destination de l'Inde – cartes, guides, hôtels et restaurants, nouveautés et événements. Pour les amateurs de culture, un panorama des musées et des galeries d'art dans tout le pays.

› **indochina-services.com**
Bonne vue d'ensemble sur le Viêt Nam, le Cambodge, le Laos, Thaïlande, Indonésie et Myanmar, avec banque de données et liens vers les centres d'informations touristiques. Pour les individualistes, des adresses de voyagistes sélectionnés.

› **jnto.go.jp**
Site officiel de l'office de tourisme japonais. Bref, concis, bien organisé – même les plans des (excellentes) communications à l'intérieur du pays peuvent être consultés.

as well as trips that take you to the Philippines' past: or put together your very own adventure tour through Thailand. Put www. in front of the addresses selected on this page and click your way through the smiling countries – have a good trip!

> **luxurytravel.com**
Hotels and resorts with all the comforts, frequently prize recipients. The selection for Asia is not particularly large, but fine.

> **roughguides.com**
Next to Lonely Planet, the second largest guidebook series that also provides excellent and up-to-date information on the Internet. For every country, the rubric "Basics" is particularly good – you would be hard put to find these essential infos in a clearer or better-prepared form.

> **tajhotels.com**
One of the largest Indian hotel groups in the luxury category. With its own spa brand ("Taj Ayurveda") and its own souvenirs that can be ordered ("Taj Shopping").

> **thai-language.com**
Try to learn Thai on the Internet! Here are the most important rules and vocabulary words organized into rubrics catered to the traveller like "At the Airport", "At the Beach" and "At a Party".

> **travel-library.com/asia/**
Here journalists and private travellers present their tours of Asia in text and photos. Not always entirely up to date, but brilliantly linked and very detailed.

> **wowphilippines.com.ph**
Very good site on the Philippines. In addition to beaches, diving spots and nature reserves, there is also information on events and special tours to the various islands.

> **lonelyplanet.com**
Ausgezeichneter Online-Auftritt eines der besten Reiseführerreihen der Welt. Umfassende, aktuelle und kritische Informationen auch über alle asiatischen Ziele – so werden für Myanmar beispielsweise die »reasons to go« und die »reasons not to go« ehrlich gegeneinander abgewogen.

> **luxurytravel.com**
Hotels und Resorts mit allem Komfort und häufig preisgekrönt. Die Auswahl für Asien ist zwar nicht besonders groß, aber fein.

> **roughguides.com**
Neben Lonley Planet die zweite große Reiseführerreise, die auch im Internet exzellente und aktuelle Informationen bietet. Besonders gut ist die Rubrik »Basics« für jedes Land – übersichtlicher und besser aufbereitet findet man diesen Grundstock selten.

> **tajhotels.com**
Eine der größten indischen Hotelgruppen der Luxuskategorie. Mit eigener Wellnessmarke (»Taj Ayurveda«) und eigenen Souvenirs zum Bestellen (»Taj Shopping«).

> **thai-language.com**
Versuchen Sie doch mal, im Internet Thai zu lernen! Hier gibt's die wichtigsten Regeln und Vokabeln – zusammengestellt in reisetauglichen Rubriken wie »Am Flughafen«, »Am Strand« und »Auf der Party«.

> **travel-library.com/asia/**
Hier stellen Journalisten und Privatreisende ihre Asien-Touren in Text und Bild vor. Nicht immer ganz aktuell, aber ausgezeichnet verlinkt und sehr ausführlich.

> **wowphilippines.com.ph**
Sehr gute Seite über die Philippinen. Neben Stränden, Tauchspots und Naturschutzgebieten wird auch über Events und besondere Touren über die verschiedenen Inseln informiert.

> **lonelyplanet.com**
Remarquable apparition on-line d'une des meilleures collections de guides de voyages du monde. Des informations complètes, actuelles et critiques, également sur les pays asiatiques. En ce qui concerne le Myanmar par exemple, les raisons de s'y rendre et de s'en abstenir sont confrontées avec une grande sincérité.

> **luxurytravel.com**
Hôtels et resorts tout confort et souvent primés. En ce qui concerne l'Asie, le choix n'est pas vaste mais raffiné.

> **roughguides.com**
A côté de Lonely Planet la seconde collection de guides de voyages à offrir sur le Net des informations excellentes et mises à jour régulièrement. La rubrique « Basics » consacrée à chaque pays est particulièrement intéressante – difficile de trouver plus lisible et mieux préparé.

> **tajhotels.com**
Un des plus importants groupes hôteliers catégorie Luxe. Avec sa marque de remise en forme (« Taj Ayurveda ») et des souvenirs à commander (« Taj Shopping »).

> **thai-language.com**
Pour ceux qui essaient d'apprendre la langue Thaï sur Internet ! Les règles essentielles et le vocabulaire sont rassemblés ici dans des rubriques pratiques pour le voyageur, par exemple « A l'aéroport », « Sur la plage » et « Pendant la fête ».

> **travel-library.com/asia/**
Des journalistes et des particuliers présentent ici leurs voyages en Asie en textes et en images. Mise à jour laissant à désirer mais liens remarquables et très détaillé.

> **wowphilippines.com.ph**
Très bon site sur les Philippines. A côté des plages, des sites de plongée et des réserves naturelles, informations sur les événements et les circuits particuliers dans diverses îles.

TASCHEN Web-Tipps:
Die Zeit bis zum nächsten Urlaub ist zu lang? Dann holen Sie sich den Zauber Asiens auf den heimischen Bildschirm – mit Hilfe dieser Web-Tipps. Hier finden Sie noch mehr indische Hotelpaläste, balinesische Traumvillen und malaiische Strandbungalows, reisen in die Vergangenheit der Philippinen oder stellen sich Ihre ganz persönliche Erlebnistour durch Thailand zusammen. Setzen Sie www. vor die ausgewählten Adressen auf diesen Seiten und klicken Sie sich durch die Länder der Lächelns – gute Reise!

Les meilleurs sites web selon TASCHEN :
Les vacances vous semblent encore trop loin ? Alors faites venir chez vous l'Asie et tous ses charmes en vous aidant de nos sites recommandés. Vous y trouverez encore plus de palais indiens, de villas de rêve balinaises et de bungalows malaysiens, vous voyagerez dans le passé des Philippines ou vous organiserez votre périple personnel à travers la Thailande. Ajoutez www. devant les adresses sélectionnées et partez à la découverte des pays du sourire – bon voyage !

Photo Credits | Fotonachweis
Crédits photographiques

© 2009 TASCHEN GmbH
Hohenzollernring 53, D-50672 Köln
www.taschen.com

ORIGINAL EDITION:	© 2004 TASCHEN GmbH
EDITED AND LAYOUT:	Angelika Taschen, Cologne
GENERAL PROJECT MANAGEMENT:	Stephanie Bischoff, Cologne
LITHOGRAPH MANAGER:	Thomas Grell, Cologne
ENGLISH TRANSLATION:	Cathy Lara, Berlin
	Sophie Lovell, Berlin
FRENCH TRANSLATION:	Michèle Schreyer, Cologne
	Thérèse Chatelain-Südkamp, Cologne
DESIGN:	Lambert und Lambert, Düsseldorf
PRINTED IN	China
ISBN	978-3-8365-1481-1

To stay informed about upcoming TASCHEN titles, please
request our magazine at www.taschen.com/magazine or write
to TASCHEN, Hohenzollernring 53, D-50672 Cologne, Germany;
contact@taschen.com; Fax: +49-221-254919. We will be happy to
send you a free copy of our magazine, which is filled with information about all of our books.